Way of the Warrior 2

Bernard Schaffer

CONTENTS

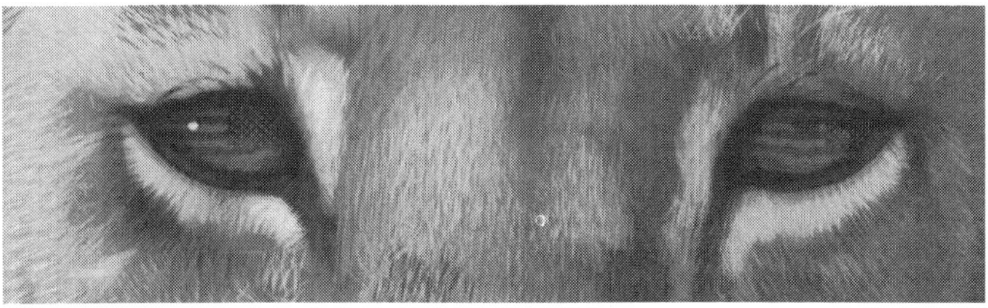

ONE: The Lion Roars

I have a confession to make. I recently changed my mind about something, because I was wrong. It all started with my ex-wife.

She and I come from very different backgrounds. I grew up in the countryside of Horsham Township in a police and hunting family. I spent my youth splashing around the muddy cornfields of Bower's Farm. I shot archery in the backyard at hay bales. There was a gun cabinet in the dining room filled with rifles and shotguns and two of them were mine.

She hated guns. Didn't want anything to do with them. She grew up in Northeast Philadelphia with parents who fancied themselves hippies. She's Jewish. Now, I'm not saying that in any kind of derogatory way, and I don't want anyone reading it to think, "Oh, she's *Jewish*. I get it."

I don't mean it like that. My kids are half-Jewish, so understand that I'm only bringing this up to point out that we come from completely different backgrounds.

I'm sort of a mutt when it comes to cultural heritage. My mom is Italian and Irish, though she never met her father. My father's dad was adopted and it was never discussed who his real father had been. Hell, for all I know, I'm Jewish too. But I grew up spending most of my holidays with the Italians, who certainly give any other culture a run for their money in terms of festivities. All the women spend two weeks cooking a hundred and fifty-two course meal that begins on a Wednesday and ends the second Sunday of the following month. You can't eat for six weeks after a proper Italian holiday dinner, which is okay, because you will be in a food coma for four and a half of them.

When my ex-wife invited me to my first Jewish holiday dinner I was ready. I was prepared. I starved myself for two days just to have the room I knew I would need to fit the smorgasbord of mysterious Jewish dishes I was about to encounter and defeat.

"What's a Pesach, anyway?" I asked her while we drove there.

"It's just a dinner," she said. "Lots of different traditional dishes. It starts off with my favorite soup in the world."

"Excellent," I said, needing to speak up to be heard over the loud rumbling of my stomach. I truthfully had no idea what traditional Jewish food was, but I didn't care. I was too busy daydreaming about this exotic soup that this captivating woman seemed to love, and after that I pictured racks of roasted lamb and mugs of good wine. I knew there were specific Jewish wines. I'd seen them in the liquor store before and never had a chance to try them, but that night, I figured I was going to drink them all.

By the time we arrived I was in a near-dizzy state of hunger and bracing myself for the endless orgy of food that was about to transpire. If little old Jewish ladies were anything like little old

Italian ladies, there would be a quick bombardment of kisses greeting us and then we would be corralled into a line of other relatives heaping a Buick sedan's worth of this glorious soup into massively oversized bowls we needed two hands to carry.

And, I'm pleased to say that they did hand me something when I walked in, although it wasn't food. It was a prayer book. A prayer books with songs and stories and a one-act play with everyone's name scribbled in beside a long section of dialogue. Now, as we sat down at the dinner table surrounded by fine china plates and linen napkins and absolutely empty drinking glasses, these people began to read the book. They began to sing the songs and pray the prayers and act out the story and I realized with trembling horror that they were going to read the entire book.

"What's wrong?" my ex whispered to me.

"Nothing," I said, smiling as best as I could. "This is great. Really. Just great."

"Is it like what your family does?"

I looked at her. "We usually say grace before the main course." I didn't mention that this was after an hour of eating and that my grandmother was already half-drunk. Which, I might add, made for some pretty interesting graces.

After the final passage was read, it was time to play a game. They brought in bowls of hard-boiled eggs that everybody picked up and started smacking together, seeing who could crack the other person's egg first. When my ex turned toward me with her egg in hand, ready to do battle, her look of eagerness became confusion. I had already cracked my egg open and eaten half of it. "You weren't supposed to do that," she said.

I apologized as I ate the rest of it. I waited for her and her cousin to smash their eggs together. My ex lost and dropped her broken egg in her bowl and watched the rest of her family compete. She didn't seem to mind, so I ate her egg too.

And then it was time for the soup I'd heard so much about. Everyone at the table seemed genuinely pleased when the soup was being brought in, and for the first time that evening, I was beginning to feel like things were looking up. "Have you ever had matzo ball soup, Bernard?" her mother asked me.

"No, but I've heard a lot about it," I said, nodding eagerly.

The first ladle full had nothing but clear broth. And the next, and the next, and the next. Finally, she plunked down a golf-ball size hunk of matzo that looked like wet dough and said, "Enjoy."

I ate every tiny bit of that dough ball and drank all the broth. I finished my ex's broth and her cousin's dough ball too. They brought out crackers and some kind of bitter purple paste, and I ate that too. My ex looked at me and said, "You ate the maror? I can't even eat that."

"I'm eating everything they put in front of me," I muttered.

Then they brought out plates of gefilte fish. Now, I've been around fish my whole life. I've fished streams and ponds and lakes and the Atlantic Ocean and I've caught everything from big blue fish to eels and I have never, ever, heard of anyone catching a gefilte fish. My ex scowled at the pickled clump of gray fish-matter in front of us and said, "Don't even think about it."

Everybody else on our side of the table seemed to be thinking the same thing, because nobody moved. At the other end of the table, the older folks were digging in. "Old folks must know more than us because they've been on the planet so much longer," I thought to myself, and I picked up a fork and speared myself a gefilte fish.

Now, I'm not sure how to describe what it's like to eat a mouthful of cold pickled fish that's been ground up and reconstituted into a sliver of fish cake bathed in gel, but as I took that first bite, every single person at the table turned to look at me. No one spoke as I sat there chewing. Once I finally managed to swallow, the grandmother at the table smiled and said, "How do you like it?"

"So good," I muttered, feeling the fish goo roiling in my guts and cold slimy bits coating my teeth. I laid down my fork and said, "But I need to save room now. I'm getting stuffed on all this good food."

"All right, dear," the old lady said. "We'll make sure you get some to take home."

Now, over the years, I got to know many members of her family and as far as I know, none of them had ever been police officers. None of them hunted. None of them ever served in the military. None of them were ever fire fighters. It was simply not part of her family's culture, and because of that, she never understood many of the things that went with it. Most of all, she never understood guns.

In her mind, by insisting that guns be kept away from her and the kids, it will keep them safe. In her mind, by refusing to even discuss them, it means they don't exist. She absolutely refused to let me carry a gun off duty. And you know what? I listened.

Now, I know more than a few of you card-carrying NRA members are rolling your eyes right now and calling me all sorts of names, but let me explain myself. I was married to a woman who became so insanely upset at the prospect of me carrying a gun that it was easier to lock the damn thing up and leave it at home than put my foot down. I picked the path of least resistance. I know I'm not the first man who caved on something to keep his wife from nagging him, but one thing I pride myself on is that I tell the truth. Even when it doesn't make me look good, I tell it, and here it is. I stopped carrying a gun off duty because it upset my ex-wife.

To be honest, I didn't miss it that much. Carrying a gun around is a pain in the ass, really. You have to always worry about wearing clothes that cover it up. They're heavy. They're awkward. There's a better chance of losing it than if it were locked up at your house or police station. And best of all, you have an excuse for not getting involved.

You see, one thing I've come to realize is that when I lock my gun up at home instead of carrying it, I'm secretly locking up my responsibility as a police officer. If someone does something horrible in front of me and I back away with the rest of the crowd, if I choose to stand on the sidelines instead of joining the fray, I can always say, "Sorry, folks. I didn't have my gun on me."

Strangely enough, I always carried a badge though. I'd sooner walk out of the house naked than forget my badge. Of course, I wasn't carrying the badge to be of use to anybody but me. God forbid I had to identify myself to another police officer, I was going to need that magic piece of tin to show that I was one of the good guys. But a gun? Weren't we all taught the same thing in the police academy?

"Be a good witness."

I can be a great witness. I'm a trained observer. I will get you a description of the bad guy that would make his mother cry. I can write your police report for you, plus, I know how to testify. And if my only area of responsibility during an incident is to be a good witness, what the hell do I need a gun for?

And so, even though my ex-wife and I have been divorced for years, I never carried a gun after that either, especially when I had the kids because I was afraid it would cause problems. I picked the illusion of safety over the actual safety of the most precious people in my life.

We all know that guy.

His pants have too many pockets. He's got a funny haircut. He's the gun nut. The one who won't cut his grass without a .357 tucked inside his jean shorts. The paranoid freak who spends too much time watching Fox News and stocks up on ammo and canned goods. The person who still wears a fanny pack. Or ever wore a fanny pack, for that matter.

On the street, that is the guy we don't want to run into. He's the one we think must be using a gun to supplement some other kind of shortcoming. The guy buying more assault weapons than our SWAT team has, and tricking them out better, too.

Nobody wants to be that guy, but I'm sure we can all agree they are out there. I'm sure we can all agree that it's fun to tease them and hold ourselves up as more sophisticated and less gullible than they are, right?

Right up until you're walking with your family at the Clackamas Town Center and a maniac in a hockey mask steps out with a Bushmaster M4 and starts gunning people down. Two people died as a result of that rampage.

Right up until you're sitting inside the Century movie theater watching Dark Knight Rises and a maniac wearing a gas mask and helmet enters the theater and starts shooting. Twelve people died that time.

And as I think about these things, the fundamental question I must ask myself and you is, in that situation, am I supposed to be a good witness? Am I supposed to watch innocent women and children get gunned down in front of me because the only thing I was prepared to do that day was be a good witness? No. Not just no, a resounding no. A heartfelt no from the depths of my being that says not while I'm here, not while it is my time to hold this line, and not while it is yours either.

I'm going to lose a few of you when I say this next part, and that's all right. I respect that people have strong beliefs that are different than mine, and if you can't tolerate my point of view that the NRA is bad for America, then so be it. I do not believe that every citizen in this country deserves or needs to have every sort of firearm under the sun. I do not believe that is what the Second Amendment intended, and I think the NRA has exploited people in order to increase their political and financial power.

Now as I say this, I'm thinking about my dad and uncles and grandparents, all of whom are lifetime members of the NRA. They get the magazine, the membership card, the bumper stickers, and so on. Some of them are turning over in their graves right now as I write these words, but I write them because I believe them to be true.

However, all that being said, I do not believe gun control would have any meaningful effect on reducing mass shootings either. So, while I will not be attending any NRA fundraisers in the foreseeable future, I am also not drinking the gun control Kool-Aid. I've done enough research on the subject to realize that gun control will not prevent homicidal maniacs from acquiring whatever weapons they can.

Like many of you, I'm somewhere in the middle. It's the same way I feel about most any of the hot button political issues. Abortion, welfare, health care, immigration, and so on. Put me under the hot light and interrogate me about any one of those issues and I'll eventually say, "Sometimes, I guess so. Maybe not in others."

In my opinion, too many groups profit from shoving too many middle of the road Americans from one side or another. I am not an extremist. I shouldn't be forced to declare allegiance to one extreme faction that espouses things I do not believe.

And the reason I say all of this is because I want to make it very clear that my avocation of carrying a gun off duty has nothing to do with the second amendment. If anything, my choice to always be armed has been bolstered by the fact that groups like the NRA and their political cronies have succeeded in flooding this country with high-power firearms, and our enemies can acquire them with ease.

Now, as I say this, some of you are weeping openly into your NRA logo tissues and getting ready to either toss this book in the trash or find the nearest gun owner forum and talk smack about your friendly neighborhood crime fighting author. That really is okay. I didn't come to pander to any group or particular point of view. There is enough of that in modern media, and personally, I don't trust anyone who bows to a large organization and says, "They speak for me and I agree with everything they say."

Since I started carrying regularly, my family has noticed, and it's given us a chance to talk about situations that might not come up otherwise. The other day, I took my kids to a school fair. It was a gorgeous spring day after a week of solid rain fall. The sun was high, and there was a cool breeze filled with the scent and taste of spare ribs, and chicken wings, and popcorn. What kind of a person brings a gun with him to an elementary school fair? What would people say if they knew I was armed? What kind of father was I being? For a moment, I felt almost embarrassed as I strapped on my belt and holster.

The real answer is different from the kind and gentle answer. The kind and gentle answer is we're just going to a fun-filled day of bouncy castles and cotton candy. My kids want to run around playing games, winning cheap plastic trinkets and seeing if they can plop a ping-pong ball into a small fishbowl. The kind and gentle answer is that shooting someone in the middle of a school fair should have been the farthest thing from my mind.

Unless you think about the possibilities.

First, we all know all schools discourage the carrying of firearms or other weapons on their property, and in some states, it is illegal. So there is a lack of legitimate defensive weapons available.

Second, the people in attendance at these events are families and young children. Let's see, who can we think of that would view families and children as a high-value target? Especially a large cluster of them that would guarantee maximum media coverage if they were injured, maimed, or killed? I could write a thousand words on the kinds of individuals and organizations that are drooling like hyenas at the thought of it, and I still wouldn't cover all the bases.

Third, the revenge scenario where an estranged domestic partner shows up and decides to even the score by blowing away the people who caused them pain.

Four, the availability of cops at events like these are minimal. There is normally an ambulance, and possibly private security, but as far as properly equipped and trained and armed law enforcement personnel? Hardly ever. In fact, it's been my experience that most schools and public events eschew having uniformed cops present because it gives the illusion of an un-safe environment.

"Why are the cops here?"

"Are you expecting trouble?"

"Is there something I need to know about?"

"I don't want to see someone with a gun at my child's school when I'm here with my family, just trying to have a good time."

And if you think that the bad guys haven't figured all this out, you are fooling yourself. You are sticking your head into the sand and burying it as deeply as you can, all because you are choosing to bathe in those lukewarm waters of indifference and naivety. They know all of this, they are actively planning to take advantage of all of this, and we are not prepared to deal with the results. We are showing our bellies to these snarling dogs and saying, "Please don't hurt us, we pose no threat to you." But these dogs have no mercy and they will tear you and your children apart if you let them.

The real truth is that no one else is going to save you in time.

The real truth is that the shit will hit the fan so fast and so hard that the only possible person who can save all those innocent lives is a trained warrior on-scene who cared enough to bring a gun that day.

Do you love your family enough to carry a gun with you everywhere you go? Even if nothing ever happens and all it does is mean you have to spend the rest of your life clothes shopping in the men's "tactical" aisle?

Now let me ask you this. Do you love my family enough to do the same? Do you love every family at that shopping mall, at that school fair, at that movie theater, to do the same? Do you love all these little kids running around with no idea that there are sick, evil, highly-motivated people coming for them at any given moment, and are you ready to engage those people and neutralize the threat?

Do you love this country enough to do that?

Those kids, you see, are not the actual target. They're the victims, certainly, but they're not the actual target. They're a means to an end for the terrorist or mass shooter to achieve their disgusting fantasy of receiving attention for killing babies. They want America as a whole to suffer. They want America to cease to exist, and they are crawling all over us like viruses.

They know they can use our own freedoms against us, our own hard won constitutional protections to get weapons and carry out their horrible plans.

They know our military cannot fight on American soil. They know that most police departmental organizations are understaffed, underfunded, underequipped and unprepared to deal with an immediate threat the moment it happens.

They know all these things and they train with them in mind and they are preparing right now to exploit our vulnerabilities. They are coming for our children.

But here is what they do not know.

We have seven hundred and eighty thousand police officers in the United States, in the homeland, living in our communities. In addition to that, there are one hundred and twenty thousand armed federal agents. We have an elite fighting force of men and women who are trained to deal with anything we encounter, or at the very least, defend our citizens until the rest of the team gets there. But only if they are equipped and prepared and properly motivated.

I'll ask you again. Do you love this country enough to defend what we have?

I think you do. I think you're reading this book right now nodding your head because you know that not only does the true blue line extend from sea to sea and border to border, it is woven into the fabric of this nation as surely as the blue field displayed on every American flag since the seventeen hundreds.

Vigilance, perseverance, and justice.

Did you know those are the characteristics attributed to Old Glory Blue? Could there be any more apt description for the warriors who take an oath upon their shield to serve and protect? Vigilance, perseverance, and justice. I say we need it now as much as it was needed when we battled the British Empire for freedom or the Axis of Evil to save the world from a menace that tried to snatch the light from our existence.

In 2011, an imam from the Al-Aqsa mosque in Pakistan made headlines. It was shortly after the United States had captured and killed Osama Bin-Laden, and the imam posted a YouTube video claiming the bodies of Presidents Obama and Bush would hang for their crime. He called us dogs, and said, "Dogs should not rejoice too much for killing lions."

You know, American history can be a funny thing.

If you read some of the newer conservative books on history, you'd think our founding fathers were saints. If you read Howard Zinn's books, you'd think they were all a pack of slave-raping land hoarders. Like all things, the truth is probably somewhere in the middle.

It is undeniably true that the American federal government has done some incredibly destructive, ill-advised things to various countries in the course of our history. I'm not denying that, I'm not white-washing that, and I'm not excusing it. We have some stains upon our honor and it does us no good to lie about it.

We are not alone among countries that have committed horrific deeds, and ours might pale in comparison to those done by many others, but that excuses nothing. We can, and should, do better.

Slavery is, and always will, be one of the darkest marks on American history. We did wrong, and we are still dealing with the consequences of our ancestors' actions to this day as a result of it. However, what is often not mentioned is that slavery existed since pre-historic times, and that in the era that America was founded, it existed in every major country around the world. But only one went to war to end it. Only one was willing to fight and sacrifice and die to stamp out that most insipid kind of evil.

Dogs?

There were eight hundred and thirty-eight attacks on Pakistani schools between 2009 and 2012 by their own countrymen. At least thirty children were killed and almost a hundred more were injured by their own countrymen.

Dogs?

In 2010, thirty-one percent of a sample group of Pakistani citizens reported they'd paid bribes to local police. That doesn't include the bribes they also reported paying to judges, prosecutors, hospital staff, and utility workers.

We're the dogs?

In World War I we sacrificed over fifty-three thousand American soldiers in combat, and in World War II we sacrificed a staggering two hundred and ninety one thousand five hundred and fifty seven more. We are the reason everybody else on that side of the planet doesn't speak German right now, so do not call dare us dogs.

When you speak of the warrior class that exists in the United States of America, you better understand you are speaking of lions.

Ladies and gentlemen reading this book, this is our jungle. It's bigger than your precinct, your district, your township, your sector, your neighborhood, and your home. We do not have the luxury of waiting for the politicians to magically fix the problem. We do not have the luxury of waiting for the cops on duty or SWAT to show up and suppress and defeat the problem. It might be terrorists, or it might be a psychotic gunman, or it might be anything else under the sun, but one thing is certain: They want to hurt us. As a country. As a populace. As a way of life.

They are training to hurt us. They are preparing to hurt us. They are actively readying an assault on our most vulnerable citizens as we speak, and it is our job to meet them with a wall of blue fire. A fire that will burn long after all of us are gone.

When I stopped carrying my gun off duty, I stepped away from that fight. When you go into a public place, and you aren't paying attention to what's happening, or you are determined to only be a good witness, or you are refusing to get involved, or you are neglecting to carry your weapon, you are stepping away from that fight and letting the enemy run us over.

The bell has rung and it's a new round. I'm back at the front line with you now. I'm ready and equipped to do whatever it takes to defend my family, your family, and this country. I won't ever let you down again.

TWO: On Edged Weapons

I grew up carrying knives. I carried them around in my pocket whenever I went out into the fields. I used them to whittle sticks and cut through brush or dig up roots. I would ding up the blades so badly that I'd have to sharpen them on one of those tiny whetstones that came with survival knives. Remember them? They were useless pieces of knobby stone no bigger than a domino bone.

I still have a scar across the knuckle of my left middle finger from sharpening a knife with one of those. I'll never forget that day. I cut myself so deep the skin of my knuckle flopped over, pearl white on the underside. As soon I let my hand drop, blood started streaming out of it. That scar is just above the ones from the box cutter that I talked about in the last Way of the Warrior. My left arm looks like a battle-scarred veteran of bladed combat, and my right arm doesn't have a scratch on it. I bet my left arm makes fun of my right arm for being a sissy when I'm not paying attention.

My father bought me my first knife, a Schrade lockback folder with a wooden handle and brass fittings, when I was a kid. This is back when all Imperial Schrade knives were made in Ellenville, New York. That factory has since been bought out and now all manufacturing is done in Asia.

I still have the knife and the brown leather sheath it came in. That old knife was the first of many American made blades that I've continued to collect over the years. Lately, I've been focusing on W.R. Case knives because not only are they an American company that dates back to the 1800's, they are located right here in the Commonwealth of Pennsylvania.

I scour all kinds of flea markets and garage sales for anything that says Case. The nice ones, I put away for safekeeping, but I buy the dinged up ones too. I like to carry them around and use them in ways I'm too afraid to with the more collectible ones or the factory sharpened blades that I don't want to dull. Packages, boxes, packing tape, you name it. All fall victim to the old Case Sodbusters and Trappers I carry around. And people don't mind when you pull out an old folder and pry it open, at least not the same way they do when you activate a gnarly-looking serrated tactical blade that's the size of a machete. Old American-made knives have a classic, gentlemanly-quality to them and carry some of our history in their making.

Don't let a little rust or wear and tear fool you. Those boys back in Ellenville, NY, and Bradford, PA, knew how to make fine cutting tools that were meant to last. They'd use good American steel that could hold an edge. With a little bit of oil and refurbishment, a little commitment and resolve, you can take something that looks old and worn out and give it new life. Make it sharp again. Give it a renewed purpose.

And if you suspect I might be talking about something besides knives now, well, I won't tell if you don't.

In the police academy, I sat next to a knife guy. He was the first one I ever met, and his bizarre fascination with knives struck me as eccentric and sociopathic. He carried a Spyderco with the nastiest edge I'd ever seen and he'd talk all the time about "The Blue Worm."

He take the knife out and wave it slowly sideways and say, "When you cut somebody across the stomach, the biggest intestine that spills out of them is called the blue worm. All that cold air rushes into their stomach and they panic because it hurts so bad, and they immediately grab their guts and try to stuff the blue worm back inside. Then, while they're holding their stomach with both hands, you cut them across the throat."

"Stay the hell away from me with that thing," I'd say.

"A knife is the deadliest weapon in existence, if you know how to use it."

"I'd rather have a gun."

"A knife guy can kill a gun guy before he ever has the chance to draw."

"A bullet can shoot somebody from farther away than a knife. Unless you throw it or something. Do you throw your knives?"

"Only if I have more than one." And then he looked at me and said, "And yes, I always have more than one."

Sitting next to him was like sitting next to Bubba in Forrest Gump, except instead of talking about shrimp, he talked about knives.

"Did you ever train with a whip?"

"No."

"If you tie a knife to the end of a whip, it's an awesome weapon. You can snap it, flick it, slice it, all from ten feet away."

"Can you blue worm them?"

He thought it over. "Probably not. But you could cut them a few times enough to get close and lollipop them."

"What the hell does 'lollipop them' mean?"

"You thrust the knife up through the lower jaw, all the way up to the handle. When it sticks out, it looks like a lollipop."

I scowled and said, "There is something seriously wrong with you. How did you pass the psychological to get in here?"

He shrugged nonchalantly, "You can't learn how to defend yourself from a knife unless you know how to use one. You study Wing Chun, right?"

I told him I did.

"Can you use it in real life?"

"Some of it, I guess. I hope so."

"It's an art form. It's good exercise. It's fun, pretty to watch, just like all the other martial arts out there. That's all well and good." He touched the knife on his side and said, "I study how to fight with knives. They only thing it is useful for is killing someone who is trying to kill you."

Killing someone seemed like an extreme and deranged thing to study. At that point in my life I'd studied several martial arts for extensive periods of time, and none of them mentioned killing anybody. If anything, that was frowned upon. In every martial arts movie, when the hero was surrounded by a group of thugs, he side kicked his way out of the situations. He didn't pull out a knife and start blue worming people.

It seemed to contradict everything I'd ever known, read, or loved about studying martial arts. Yet, the simple truth is this. All things being equal, a man with decades of training in empty hand combat will die or be horribly mutilated by someone with a knife. Maybe not in all circumstances, but in most.

Every martial arts or self-defense magazine in the world has an article on "How to Defend Yourself from a Knife Attack" and it shows wonderfully framed pictures of a high-block that stops an overhead attack, or a low X-block that defeats a thrust to the stomach. It is simply not reality and you can tell all the martial arts instructors in the world that I said so.

There are many wonderful advantages to studying every martial art in the world. People who study Tai Chi might relax better and people who study Tae Kwon Do can perform a series of beautiful kicks in an amazing display of athletic ability. But people who train in knife combat train for one thing. Killing people who are trying to kill them.

After almost ten years of training with knives, I can say that it is an ugly, ghoulish thing to practice techniques that teach you to stab another person. To map the human anatomy in terms of vital targets such as the femoral arteries and eyes and attack them first. Knife combat is neither honorable, nor fair, not in any sense of the word, and it is not good for any other thing except ending a fight. Permanently.

In the last Way of the Warrior, I touched on the subject of off-hand carry for duty knives. As you may recall, I said that officers who carry a knife on the same side as their gun hand are not thinking clearly if they intend to deploy that knife as a method of weapon retention. I should have mentioned that it is equally important to keep your knife on your off-hand side when you are not working. That you must train with it on that side. Train in opening it, deploying it, and using it as necessary. If you are right handed in life, you have to become a left handed knife fighter.

In knife combat, it is said that the hand with the knife does not kill you, the empty hand does. The empty hand clears the path for the blade to find its target. In reality, knife fighters train with a blade in each hand, so it really doesn't matter. A pass or a grab that would occur with the empty hand becomes a pass or a grab with a bladed hand just as easily, but instead of using your fingers to hold onto your opponent, you use a knife.

Over the years, I've been extremely fortunate to train with titans of edged weapon combat. Tuhon Tom Kier of Sayoc Kali, Rob Walker of Combative Edge, and Grand Tuhon Leo Gaje Jr. of Pekiti Tirsia Kali, and many others have all contributed to my better understanding of exactly how deadly and effective knives are. I am not an expert, by any means. I know enough to understand how much I do not know.

A warrior should be intimately familiar with every piece of equipment he or she carries. If you are carrying a knife, you must study it, train with it, and use it. Otherwise, you are carrying it for show and it is a useless as the officer who brings a bullet proof vest on patrol every day and leaves it in the car.

"Use it?" you say.

I realize many of you are carrying very expensive knives that you don't want to risk damaging, but that is like carrying a gun you are afraid to shoot. Shooters have to use their weapons to understand them. How many times have you practiced drawing your gun, firing it, reloading it, and clearing jams over the course of your career? Hundreds, if not thousands of times, until you know how to expect that weapon to perform when you use it.

My personal opinion is that if you are carrying a five hundred dollar knife around that you refuse to use because you are "saving it" for when you need it, it is a very expensive piece of decoration. You are choosing form over function, Jean-Claude Van Damme.

There is a multitude of live blade cutting drills people perform that you can choose from. The most realistic ones seem to use the carcasses of dead pigs or sides of beef where people stab and slice with wild abandon. While I can see the value in that as a one-time thing, it doesn't seem very practical on a regular basis. And seriously, who is cleaning all that up?

My preferred cutting drills involve plastic containers of various shapes and sizes. I take an assortment of soda bottles or gallon-sized jugs and fill them up with water. The water adds weight to the bottles and gives an accurate idea of the damage you inflict.

I tie each of the bottles to a tree branch at varying heights, and run timed drills to see how quickly I can make a single bottle empty or how many bottles I can puncture. Before any of you runs out and tries this, let me warn you, this is more dangerous than it sounds.

Start off slowly, with just one bottle, and practice until you are proficient. Always bear in mind that you are now swinging a live blade at a moving target in a very wet environment. If you are using your empty hand to steady the bottle before you strike it, you run a real risk of impaling yourself through the hand or arm. So don't.

Take your empty hand and press it against your chest to keep it out of the way.

Live blade training will give you a very quick understanding of the weapon you are using and how much it needs to be respected. I used to carry a Gerber Fairbairn Applegate folder, and I loved that blade. It had a thin, sleek profile, and was razor sharp. It wasn't until I used the knife in several drills that I realized it had a notch in the handle that cut me every time I stuck it into something. It is a flaw that I never would have noticed unless I'd actually used it. I am sure you can imagine that having an open wound in your hand is not a great idea when you have to deploy your blade at a human target who may or may not carry a whole host of communicable diseases.

If you grow bored of using plastic bottles, you can try old car tires or ropes or many other materials that will test both the weapon and the warrior. Be sure to practice with both hands and to use the same amount of care and safety precautions as you would when shooting at the range. Since the days when early man first learned to fashion tools out of stones and sticks, the edged weapon has been a source of survival. It is a primitive thing of such perfect design that it has not needed to evolve much since the days when we all lived in caves.

THREE: Reassessing Rampage Killers

One of the things I admire most about science is that nothing can be presented as legitimate unless it is tested, replicated, and reviewed by panels of peers. Very prominent scientific figures have been forced to back away from their positions on various topics and admit they were wrong. The thing the scientific community has learned, in ways that other powerful movements have not, say for example, religion, is that being wrong is okay. Being disproven is embraced. When someone provides evidence that a long-held belief is inaccurate, it is greeted with gratitude.

Now, the evidence has to be actual evidence. It can't be based on circular logic or the assertion of opinion, no matter how old or sacred that opinion is believed to be.

For instance, in 2004, renowned physicist Stephen Hawking revealed that he was mistaken in various parts of his theories relating to black holes. He reversed a position he'd held since the 1970s regarding matter being consumed by black holes, and a few other things that I am not really qualified to relate back to you here.

In 2014, Hawking again stirred debate when he came forward to say he was not certain black holes even existed. Or if they do, it is not in any of the ways that modern physics theorists, a majority of whom based their research on what Hawking had been espousing since the 1970s, understood.

When is the last time in history you can remember a famous public figure outside of the realm of science saying anything remotely close to that?

In our own way, police investigators are scientists, and we are bound by the same commitment to factual, provable results that can withstand scrutiny. In elementary school, we all learned the Scientific Method and were taught to follow these steps:

1. Ask a Question
2. Conduct Background Research on Your Subject
3. Construct a Hypothesis
4. Test the Hypothesis through Experimentation
5. Analyze the Data and Draw a Conclusion
6. Report the Results

Too often, in every level of government, we back ourselves into corners with initiatives or procedures that simply do not work, but because of ego or stubbornness, we are forced to ride that pony regardless of how crippled or awkward it is. If you've ever heard the phrase, "This is the way we do it because this is the way we've always done it," you understand what I'm talking about.

In the first Way of the Warrior book, I warned you about the dangers of developing a theory to fit the crime and then trying to shoehorn all of your results into that theory. I told you to follow the evidence and organically develop a suspect, or else you risked tainting your results. If we hold up the Scientific Method as the framework for our finding of fact, we arrive at much cleaner, more reliable results.

If you have done your job properly, it doesn't mean you will have an unblemished track record of cases closed by arrest or guilty jury verdicts. Not every case is a winner, and it is equally as important to exonerate the innocent man when he is accused of a crime as it is to prosecute the guilty.

Your credibility as a police officer is based on your ability to tell the truth, and that applies to you whether you are an academy cadet or the Director of the FBI. Not just telling the truth when it is convenient, or advantageous, or casts you in a positive light. Any idiot can do that. It lies in your ability to tell the truth when it invalidates your ticket, or blows your case, or revokes a policy you implemented.

Always, always, always tell the truth. Tell it first, and tell it loud, and do not couch it with weasel-mouthed excuses. It sounds like such a simple thing, but happens far too infrequently.

On December 14, 2012, I was doing the same thing you were, watching in absolute horror at the news reports describing the Sandy Hook Elementary School shooting. I still cannot wrap my mind around the events of that day. I still cannot grasp what those poor, innocent babies and teachers went through that day, or what their families suffered.

Like many Americans, I raised my voice to cry out for gun control.

It was the first time I'd dipped my toes into the murky water of that particular topic and I was immediately astounded at how rabidly either side defends their position. An interesting thing happened to me along the way, however. As I began to research the topic, looking to bolster my position on why gun control was necessary to reduce mass tragedies, I realized I was wrong.

The data did not support my position.

I began with a question. Many questions, actually. By being true to the steps of the scientific method, and following the evidence like a trained, impartial investigator, I realized gun control would have little to no effect on reducing tragedies like Sandy Hook.

Now, before my NRA friends start high-fiving each other that I'm finally starting to make sense, let me be clear. I do not believe the citizens of the United States need to possess military-grade rifles or ammunition. I do not believe that is what the founding fathers intended, I do not believe that is what the 2nd Amendment was written for, and just because you think something is cool and you feel entitled to have it, doesn't mean you should.

Furthermore, I do not see anything wrong with insisting that people looking to purchase a gun have to pay for and pass both a psychological exam and training curriculum on firearm use and safety. These training curriculums could include safety, storage, scenarios, and legal information that could prove truly beneficial to the gun owners. Information they can receive from responsible, qualified trainers, as opposed to a variety of other, less rational sources online.

For the National Rifle Association to take the position that any attempt to regulate guns is an assault on freedom is nothing but scare-tactic propaganda and panders to the worst instincts of the American public.

The assertion that "Spree Killers" or "Rampage Killers" who commit acts of mass murder are an American phenomenon, or a new phenomenon, are mistaken. Of the ten worst atrocities committed by a single gunman that resulted in mass casualties, only three were committed on American soil. The earliest ones we have record of occurred in 1927 and 1938. Six incidents were perpetrated with what are commonly called "Assault Rifles" and all but two used weapons or materials that legally belonged to the suspects.

The following list provides information on the ten worst incidents in modern history. Lists like this have to be used sparingly, because they are highly attractive to potential killers. Whereas a normal human being would read these atrocities and feel sickened by the loss of innocent lives, these people see a body count score that they want to beat.

It is vital for us to understand these previous incidents, because these are the battle plans a future Adam Lanza or Eric Harris. They will review these incidents the way you and I would review a previous investigation, looking to build on what worked before and modify their approach. We can mine them for data of our own.

1. Anders Behring Breivik

Year: 2011

Country: Norway

Weapon: Ruger Mini-14 Carbine, Glock 34 pistol

Location: Oslo government building and Utoya Island at the Norwegian Labor Party Youth Camp

Killed: 77

Injured: 242

Anders Behring Breivik killed seventy-seven people on July 22nd, 2011. At approximately 3:25 PM that day, he detonated a bomb at the Regjeringskvartalet, a cluster of buildings in central Oslo, Norway, where several of Norway's government offices are stationed. The bomb was composed of a mixture of fertilizer and fuel and placed inside a car that Breivik parked in front of the building. Eight people were killed and nine were seriously injured.

Breivik then dressed up in a self-made police uniform and drove to a ferry that would take him to the island of Utoya. Utoya was the location of that Norwegian Labour Party's AUF youth camp, and approximately six hundred people were on the island at the time. Breivik identified himself as a police officer and said he was there to protect the inhabitants after the Oslo attack. This ruse allowed him to be taken to the island by ferry, where he began executing people almost immediately.

From 5:17 PM to 6:30 PM, Breivik walked around the island killing at will. He murdered sixty-nine people, and injured one hundred and ten more. Of those injured, fifty-five were considered gravely wounded.

Anders Behring Breivik surrendered to police at Utoya and has been in custody ever since. He was declared legally sane in a 2012 criminal hearing and received a twenty-one year prison term, although the sentence can be extended indefinitely if he is still considered a threat. Norway does not have the death penalty.

In the court hearing, Breivik stated that his acts were done out of "necessity" to combat the "Islamization" of Norway.

As of this writing, he is currently enrolled at the University of Oslo, studying political science from the confines of his prison cell.

Breivik began planning the massacres as early as 2002, developing a nine-year plan to finance, train, and accumulate the weapons and explosives he would need. He acquired multiple credit cards and claims to have saved over three hundred thousand dollars by 2008. In 2009 he founded a farming company and purchased a farm in Hedmark County, near the city of Oslo. Through the farm, he would acquire massive amounts of fertilizer and various chemicals that would eventually be used to create explosives.

Breivik's attacks were based on a complicated series of far right-wing ideologies that included hatred of Marxism, multiculturalism, globalization, the "Eurabia" phenomenon (thought to be the taking over of Europe by Islam), and feminists.

2. Woo Bum-Kon

Year: 1982

Country: South Korea

Weapon: Two M2 carbines, hand grenades

Location: Villages in Uiryeong County, Gyeongsangnam-do

Killed: 56

Injured: 34-37

Woo was a police officer with the South Korean police and former Marine. After a violent domestic argument with his girlfriend, he went to the local military reservist's armory and removed two rifles, ammo, and several hand grenades.

Woo then began killing everyone he encountered. He used his credentials and authority as a police officer to enter homes and businesses and then executed the people inside. He eventually barricaded himself inside a farmhouse, surrounded by the family who lived there. When the police arrived, Woo detonated two hand grenades, killing himself and most of his hostages.

3. Andrew Philip Kehoe

Year: 1927

Country: USA

Weapon: Explosives (Including dynamite and homemade firebombs)

Location: Bath Consolidated School

Killed: 44

Injured: 58

Kehoe was a farmer who became involved in local Michigan politics. He served as Treasurer of the Bath Consolidated School Board, and then Clerk for Bath Township. He was defeated during a reelection campaign for the Clerk's position in 1926.

In May 1927, his wife returned home from the hospital where she was regularly being treated for tuberculosis. Kehoe killed her two days later and proceeded to blow up his home and buildings around the farm using an assortment of dynamite, firebombs, and an explosive called pyrotol. He then detonated an explosive at the Bath Consolidated School where children attended from second to sixth grade.

The explosion killed multiple students and teachers, and emergency services personnel rushed toward the devastation. Kehoe then loaded up his truck with explosives and shrapnel material and drove it toward a crowd of people gathered at the scene. He then shot the truck with a rifle and blew it up, killing himself and several others in the process.

4. Martin John Bryant

Year: 1996

Country: Australia

Weapon: Colt AR-15 SP1 Carbine, L1A1 SLR

Location: Port Arthur Historical Site

Killed: 35

Injured: 23

Martin Bryant was an extremely troubled youth growing up in the Tasmanian suburbs. Psychologists diagnosed him with a variety of anti-social, learning, and mental disorders, and mention his inclination to torture animals.

In a strange twist of fate, at nineteen years old, Bryant befriended an eccentric older woman named Helen Harvey. Harvey was heiress to a small fortune and lived in a rundown mansion, and Bryant became her companion, spending the next several years accompanying her on shopping sprees and living the life of a wealthy young man of leisure.

Still, there were troubles. Bryant tormented his neighbors by shooting pellet guns at them or their dogs, or snatching the steering wheel whenever Harvey was driving. It is unknown whether or not he grabbed the wheel on October 20, 1992, but whatever the reason, Helen Harvey swerved head on into an oncoming car. She was killed in the collision, and Bryant suffered severe neck and back injuries. Two months later, Bryant's father committed suicide. At twenty-five years old, Martin Bryant was declared the sole beneficiary of Helen Harvey's estate, receiving over five hundred thousand dollars and her properties. He also received his father's pension, valued at over two hundred thousand dollars.

He travelled extensively over the next two years, visiting as many as fourteen foreign countries, and then, in late 1995, it is said that he became suicidal and began to drink heavily. He purchased several firearms from a local gun store, including those used in the later massacre.

On April 28, 1996, Bryant drove to a neighboring Bed and Breakfast owned and operated by the Martin family. Bryant blamed the Martins for competing with his father to purchase the Bed and Breakfast, which he felt lead to the man committing suicide. Bryant entered the home and shot and stabbed Mr. and Mrs. Martin to death.

He then drove to the Port Arthur Historical Site, a former penal colony of the British Empire constructed in the 18th Century on the Tasman Peninsula. It later became a popular tourist attraction, and on the day Martin Bryant arrived, it was decorated with groups of people visiting the site and shops and eateries and local museum. Bryant entered one of the cafes and sat down to eat a meal. Upon finishing, he stood up and removed his Colt AR 15 from a bag at his side and went table to table, executing the people inside. It took him an estimated fifteen seconds to kill twelve people and injure ten others.

He then went into a nearby gift shop where several people were hiding, and executed them as well.

During the shooting, a man inside the gift shop named ***PETER NASH*** *laid down on top of his wife, Carolyn, to hide her from*

*Martin Bryant. Bryant shot **NASH** through the neck and killed him, but he died successfully saving his wife and preventing her from being injured.*

By the time Bryant left the gift shop and café, twenty people were dead and twelve more were injured. He then walked toward the parking lot, shooting at multiple people. He killed four more and injured an additional six.

Bryant got into his car and fled the area, driving after a group of people fleeing on foot. He saw a young mother named Nanette Mikac with her three-year-old and six-year-old daughters. Bryant stopped his car and got out. Mikac begged him, "Please don't hurt my babies." Bryant shot her in the temple and killed her, then shot the three-year-old twice, killing her as well. The six-year-old little girl ran, and Bryant gave chase. He shot the child through the neck at point blank range.

He then got back in his car and drove toward the toll booth, continuing his rampage. By the time he was finished, thirty-one people were dead and nineteen more were injured.

Bryant killed a woman at a gas station and abducted her boyfriend by forcing him into the trunk of his car. He then drove back to the Bed and Breakfast where he'd killed the Martins, firing at multiple vehicles along the way.

He took his hostage inside the home and secured the residence. It was approximately 1400 hours, less than one hour from when Bryant had arrived Port Arthur.

Police eventually located Bryant and attempted to negotiate his surrender. During the negotiations, he killed his hostage, and attempted to set fire to the house in order to create a distraction that would allow him to escape. It didn't. Bryant was burned in the fire and successfully captured by police.

Bryant is now serving thirty-five life sentences for the murders and an additional thousand years for the variety of crimes he committed that day. Since his imprisonment, he has tried to kill himself six times, including an attempt in 2007 where he cut his own throat with a razor.

Interestingly enough, there are several conspiracy theories about the Port Arthur Massacre, many of which, at least as far as I can make sense of their nonsensical ramblings, want to indicate the government is responsible because it needed a catalyst to enact new gun laws.

Australia did, in fact, change its gun laws after Martin Bryant's rampage, and limited the types of firearms that could be purchased in the country. The debate rages on as to whether these laws have had any effect, either positive or negative, on reducing violent crimes.

I just want to step in here. I'm sure it cannot be easy to have read the above details about what Martin Bryant did that day, particularly to the mother and those two little girls. Believe me, it was not easy for me to conduct the research or to write about. The heinous acts that took those children's lives is something too terrible to contemplate. And yet, it falls to us to do that.

Not because we enjoy it, or want to, or are too tough to be injured by the realization that we live on the same planet as monsters who will put a gun up to a little girl's neck and squeeze the trigger. It falls to us because we may be the only ones who can stop it from happening again.

We're only four incidents into the list of ten, and three of those involved the use of multiple sites. Breivik blew up a government building, and let's be honest, if we got that call, it would be biggest thing that's ever happened during the course of our careers. That would be the immediate focus of all of our attention and resources, a crime scene of absolute national focus. But meanwhile, his second stage of the attack was hundreds of times worse.

Who among us would be thinking about, or planning for a secondary attack? Our training for major incident responses discusses the possibility of secondary I.E.D.s that are targeted at responding units, but preparing for a second-stage attack that dwarfs the first one? I haven't seen it. It would be the equivalent of responding to the Oklahoma City Bombing only to find out that Sandy Hook is in progress only a few miles away.

What public agency is ready for that? Who among us can say they are equipped, staffed, and prepared to deal with that situation? Every time I run that scenario in my head, the only possible savior to preventing or ending that criminal event is that an armed, trained person encounters the murderer and ends the threat.

Every time you put your gun into your off duty holster to carry it to the mall or to a little league baseball game or to drop the kids off at school, I want you to think about how different things might have been for Nannette Mikac and her two little girls if any one of us had been there that day.

5. Ahmed Ibragimov

Year: 1999

Country: Russia

Weapon: Kalashnikov assault rifle

Location: Chechen village of Mikenskaya

Killed: 34-41

Injured: N/A

Details of Ibragimov's actions that day are difficult to come by. Given the political nature of the incident and highly incendiary climate, coupled with the way the Russian press operates in relationship to the government, that is not particularly surprising. What is known is that Ibragimov, a Chechen who was raised in the village of Mikenskaya, returned there and began killing Russian villagers.

For a period of an hour, he searched the village for those of Russian descent and shot them, leaving a long trail of bodies in his wake. He killed everyone he shot, finishing them off with a bullet to the head to ensure their death. His youngest victim was ten years old. His oldest was eighty-nine. The rampage only ended when he ran out of ammunition and he fled the village.

Interestingly, it was the Chechens who captured him. Two days later, a group of rebels dragged Ibragimov back to the village and handed him over to the local elders. He was handcuffed to a pole in the center of town and beaten to death by relatives of his victims with iron poles.

6. Seung-Hui Cho

Year: 2007

Country: USA

Weapon: Glock 19, Walther P22

Location: Virginia Tech

Killed: 32

Injured: 17

Seung-Hui Cho immigrated with his family to the United States when he was eight years old. His family members would later recount that they were concerned about the boy, that he seemed disaffected and removed. Cho was in eighth grade when the massacre at Columbine occurred, and wrote, for a school paper, that he wanted to repeat the massacre.

According to a 2007 article in the LA Times, the school did a curious thing. Instead of alerting the authorities, they contacted Cho's sister about the paper and relied on her to notify their parents. The parents sent Cho to a psychiatrist, who diagnosed him with a various anxiety disorders and prescribed him with medication to correct the situation. By the time he graduated high school, he was no longer under the doctor's care and no longer taking medication. He applied and was accepted to Virginia Tech and moved to the campus. By his junior year, trouble was already brewing. In 2005, after a series of stalking-related incidents and various written threats, he was declared mentally ill and admitted to the Carilion St. Albans Psychiatric Hospital in Radford, Virginia. However, upon review of his case, it was decided that Cho would be better suited for outpatient treatment and he was released the following day. According to Virginia State law, Cho was still be eligible to purchase firearms, in that he was never involuntarily committed to a mental institution. In 2007, he did. He purchased two handguns, one via the internet, and one at a firearms dealer, and began purchasing ammunition.

On April 16, 2007, at approximately 7:15 AM, Cho murdered two students in a dormitory. He then returned to his room and collected a package addressed to NBC news containing videos and assorted items he wanted them to show, and mailed it from a local post office. After he mailed the package, he walked across campus to Norris Hall, a four-story academic building, carrying a backpack filled with chains, locks, and a hammer and knife. In addition, he was carrying both handguns he'd bought, as well as nineteen additional magazines, and another four hundred rounds of ammunition.

When he arrived at the building, he chained Norris Hall's three entrances shut and placed a note on one warning people not to open it or a bomb would be detonated. And then the shootings began.

In a period of less than twelve minutes, Seung-Hui Cho fired over one hundred and seventy rounds at the students and faculty inside the school. He killed thirty people, shooting each victim at least three times. Twenty-eight of the victims suffered gunshot wounds to the head.

Cho shot himself as police made entry into Norris Hall.

Multiple people were saved from being killed that day, or saved others, because they took action instead of laying down their lives. There are two I'd like to tell you about.

Professor **KEVIN GRANATA** *was a renowned researcher in biomechanics, the effects of cerebral palsy, robotics, and more. He was married and had three children. On the day of the attack,* **GRANATA** *gathered up twenty students and hid them in his third floor office because they would be able to lock the door there. He and another professor named* **WALLY GRANT** *went downstairs toward the sound of the gunshots, and Seung-Hui Cho gunned both men down. None of the students hidden in his office were injured.*

At seventy-six years old, Professor **LIVIU LIBRESCU** *was more than simply a teacher of aeroelasticity and aerodynamics at Virginia Tech. He was a Holocaust survivor whose family had been forced into a labor camp in Romania during World War II. After the war, he went on to receive a P.H.D. in fluid mechanics from the Romanian Academy, but suffered political backlash when he disavowed the Communist Party.*

Professor **LIBRESCU** *and his wife, Marlena, eventually immigrated to Israel, and later left for the United States in order to instruct our young men and women at Virginia Tech's Department of Engineering Science and Mechanics. This is a man who spent his whole life fighting evil.*

On the morning of April 16, 2007, he would do so one last time.

As Seung-Hui Cho rampaged throughout Norris Hall, he came upon Professor **LIBRESCU'S** *classroom where twenty four people were inside, ripe for the taking. As Cho tried to enter,* **LIBRESCU** *threw* *himself in front of the door and cried out for the students to escape, yelling at them to run.*

He withstood five gunshots holding that door. Five gunshots to his body that allowed twenty-two of his students to escape through the windows. If you remember one thing from this book, remember what **LIVIU LIBRESCU** *was willing to sacrifice and endure on that day in the name of protecting the innocent.*

7. Campo Elias Delgado Morales

Year: 1986

Country: Colombia

Weapon: .32 caliber revolver and a hunting knife

Location: An apartment building and the Pizzería Pozzetto restaurant

Killed: 29

Injured: 12

The case of Campo Delgado is slightly confusing, in that various reports conflict with one another depending on their origins, and I cannot read half of them because they are in Spanish. An Associated Press report published in the Wilmington N.C. Morning-Star news, dated December 6, 1986, states that Delgado "Shot his mother, burned her body and went knocking on doors, killing whoever answered. Then he dined at a restaurant and killed 20 people there before being slain by police."

Another account states that Delgado first killed a woman and her fourteen-year-old daughter in a different apartment, by gagging them, binding them, and stabbing them repeatedly. Several mention that he may have served in the Vietnam War as a United States soldier. There were popular Colombian books and film made about the incident, and some of the discrepancies may come from them. Regardless, I cannot find sources to corroborate these accounts, so I am including the information as assertion, rather than fact.

What we can verify is that Delgado was a lonely man who blamed his mother for causing the suicide of his father. On December 4, 1986, he murdered her in at their apartment with a hunting knife, then wrapped her body in newspapers and set it on fire. He then went throughout the apartment building calling out, "Fire! Fire!" and shot five different women as they opened their doors to him. Approximately five hours later, Delgado finished a meal at an Italian restaurant called Pizzería Pozzetto and began shooting the people inside with his .32 revolver. He paused often to reload from the ammunition he'd placed in an ammo belt he was wearing and a briefcase he'd brought with him. He shot thirty-two people, killing twenty of them, inside the restaurant.

Responding officers surrounded Delgado inside the restaurant and killed him.

8. Mutsuo Toi

Year: 1958

Country: Japan

Weapon: Browning shotgun, Japanese sword, and axe

Location: Village of Kaio

Killed: 30

Injured: 3

Mutsuo Toi was a twenty-one-year old man who lived in a rural village located in Okayama, Japan. He was raised by his grandmother after both of his parents died of tuberculosis at an early age, and in a cruel twist of fate, was diagnosed with the same illness as a young adult.

Toi felt rejected by the women of his village due to his illness, and began to act disturbingly toward them. When the authorities intervened, he secretly acquired a Browning shotgun, an axe, and a katana.

On the night of the incident, he cut a power line to the village to leave it in darkness. He decapitated his grandmother with the axe, then tied two flashlights to either side of his head and began going from home to home inside the village, killing the people he felt deserved it.

It was a small village, and by dawn, Toi had killed almost half of the people who lived there. His final act was to shoot himself in the chest with the shotgun.

9. Baruch Kappel Goldstein

Year: 1994

Country: West Bank

Weapon: IMI Galil

Location: Ibrahimi Mosque

Killed: 29

Injured: 125

Baruch Goldstein was the best educated person on this list, a physician who immigrated to Israel and served in the Israeli Defense Forces. When he left the military, his views became more and more outraged toward Arabs in the area, and affiliated himself with the extremist political party, Kach.

On February 25, 1994, Goldstein dressed in his army uniform and went to the Ibrahimi Mosque in Hebron at 5:00 AM. He walked past four Israeli guards carrying an IMI Galil rifle and four magazines carrying thirty-five rounds each. He entered the mosque, and positioned himself in front of the only exit, waiting for the worshippers inside to kneel and face Mecca.

Goldstein opened fire on the crowd, killing twenty-nine people and wounding another one hundred and twenty-five.

The attack ended when one brave soul hurled a fire extinguisher at Goldstein and struck him on the head. It staggered Goldstein enough for the survivors to rush him and beat him to death.

Astonishingly, the people fleeing the mosque immediately encountered a new threat.

According to a New York Times article published on March 16, 1994, dozens of Palestinian witnesses reported that the Israeli guards in front of the building opened fire on them as they ran out. Forty individuals, many of whom were hospitalized and unable to communicate with one another, provided the same version of events: Two of the three Israeli soldiers fired in the air to try and stop the crowd from stampeding. One fired into the crowd and killed at least one person.

This was in complete contradiction to the official version of events provided by the Israeli army. They claimed that Baruch Goldstein was the only shooter and the only bullet casings found inside the building came from his gun.

Conspiracy theories and varying versions of events flew back and forth in the aftermath, and the attack set off a series of riots and the deaths of multiple Israelis and Palestinians. Sadly, it also changed the way Palestinian terror groups operated. Up until the attack by Baruch Goldstein, Hamas had never authorized a suicide attack on civilians. According to an article in Haaretz, an Israel News website, written in 2008, after the massacre at the mosque, they then ordered a series of suicide bombings that have since killed over seven hundred civilians and injured thousands more.

10. Adam Peter Lanza

Year: 2012

Country: United States

Weapon: Bushmaster XM15-E2S, Glock 20SF

Location: Sandy Hook Elementary School

Killed: 27

Injured: 2

On December 14, 2012, a twenty-year-old named Adam Lanza killed his mother while she was sleeping in bed. He then drove to Sandy Hook Elementary School and forced his way into the building by shooting through the glass panels surrounding the locked doors. He murdered twenty young school children and six adult staff members.

I keep taking breaks as I write this entire section, needing to go off and do other things to try and clear my mind. However, the little bit you read above seems to be the limit of what I can rationally explain on this particular event. Nothing will help me discuss Sandy Hook in a calm, rational voice. I'm sure it's the same for you.

We can all cognitively disassociate ourselves, to some extent, from the others on this list. Many of them happened in distant places, or so long ago that we've become used to hearing about them. I think the reason Sandy Hook is so hard to discuss is that Adam Lanza specifically targeted young children. I've been doing police work since 1997, folks. Seen a lot of stuff, and most of it wasn't nice. I've worked every kind of crime scene you can imagine, including the rape and murder of children, and I still cannot fathom what happened in Sandy Hook. I just can't. If that makes me a bad author or an unreliable narrator, so be it.

What I can talk about is **VICTORIA LEIGH SOTO**, a first-grade teacher at Sandy Hook who tried hiding her students inside her classroom. When Adam Lanza came in, she told him they were somewhere else in the school. Several kids panicked and ran for it, and Soto threw herself in front of them to shield them with her body as Lanza opened fire. A teacher's aide named **ANNE MARIE MURPHY** was also found inside the classroom, covering the body of a six-year-old little boy with her own.

Five children were murdered inside the classroom, but eleven others escaped.

I can talk about first grade teacher **KAITLIN ROIG**, who barricaded her classroom door and successfully hid the fourteen children inside. Or librarians **YVONNE CECH** and **MARYANN JACOB**, who barricaded eighteen students in a storage room. Music teacher **MARYROSE KRISTOPIK**, who hid twenty fourth graders in her room and barricaded the door, standing strong while Adam Lanza banged on the door, screaming at her to let him in.

ABBEY CLEMENTS snatched two third graders out of the hallway and hid them in her classroom. Reading specialist **LAURA FEINSTEIN** grabbed another two children and hid them under desks in her classroom. Fourth grade teacher **TED VARGA** kicked out a wooden board from one of the windows and saved three other teachers who were trapped in the lounge. School Principal **DAWN HOCHSPRUNG** and the school's psychologist **MARY**

SHERLACH both confronted Lanza at the entrance and called out warnings to their fellow teachers before being murdered.

And finally, the unknown person at the school that day who turned on the PA system. Their actions alerted the rest of the school that a maniac was loose in the building and was coming for them.

FOUR: A Study of American Mass Shootings from 1984 to 2012

While rampage killers are not a purely American phenomenon, we certainly have our share of them. They pop up like weeds throughout our history, spring boarding off of one another to create clusters of mass murders. During my research, I've found that some of the cases are so widely publicized, we already know the details by heart. Others are barely discussed.

The fundamental questions of my research were these:

- Who are these killers?
- Where do they get their weapons?
- Will banning so-called "assault weapons" put a stop to these incidents?
- Will gun control be effective in limiting the guns these maniacs can get their hands on?
- How did the incidents end?

Aside from the answers to my own questions, I've uncovered a few other things as well.

There have been several stunning acts of bravery, both by law enforcement and civilians, who made a key decision in the midst of complete chaos to act. Those individuals have been clearly spelled out so that even if the names of the diseased creatures who brought such devastation upon their communities are plastered over every internet page from here to eternity, the names of the heroes who stopped them will have a home here. We'll know who they are. If you ever get the chance to meet one, buy them a beer.

As I compiled massive amounts of data from research groups and newspaper accounts, I've determined that not everyone is on the same page. There are some glaring flaws in the way their research is presented, as well as some suspiciously absent information. My findings may deviate from the accepted academic ones, but with good reason.

Understand that incidents like these are so high profile, and so rife with speculation that a flood of varying versions of stories emerge. Now, with the internet, and a multitude of bloggers and commentators, not all of whom are people you'd want knocking on your door, facts can get very twisted, very quickly. That being said, I've done my best to corroborate the information you'll see below, but by all means, do your own research and verify what I have to say.

The Citizens Crime Commission of New York City is a non-profit, non-partisan, organization that studies crime and develops programs to reduce it. One of their areas of study was an initiative to study Mass Shootings in the United States, compiling data from 1984 to 2012.

As I researched the New York City Crime Commission's data, I was disturbed by the fact that they left several important incidents out of their reporting and that they made it a point to illustrate when the suspects had purchased their weapons legally, but not illegally.

I fail to understand the reason for one-sided reporting and my first, worst suspicion is that it is some sort of bias. I don't trust biases and they immediately put me on alert like a bloodhound picking up a scent, because if you are hedging your information about one thing, you are almost certainly doing it about something else.

The Violence Policy Center is a non-profit group based in Washington DC that has published multiple findings related to gun violence in the United States. One of their papers, "Where'd They Get Their Guns?" studied how shooters responsible for high-profile incidents.

The Violence Policy Center also does something unusual in their reporting. Multiple times, they've listed guns used in Mass Shootings as legally obtained when they were, in fact, stolen by the suspects. Usually it was when juveniles stole the firearms from their family or friends to commit school shootings. I fail to understand what the difference is between stealing a gun from a store or stranger and stealing one from your uncle or grandparent. A stolen gun is a stolen gun. Just because someone in the house legally obtained it does not mean it was there for the taking.

The New York City Crime Commission is a non-partisan group, however, the Violence Policy Center says up front that it advocates for gun control. As I said before, I do not object to the idea of gun control, particularly when it comes to providing untrained, unvetted civilians with better firepower than our police departments. That may strike many of you as heresy, but I make no secret of my personal beliefs. What I do object to is any organization bending the facts or obscuring the data to promote their own agenda.

My agenda, as you might have guessed, is understanding rampage killers and stopping them.

Using the FBI's standard of four victims or more to be classified as a Mass Shooting, there were at least fifty incidents in the United States from 1984 to 2012. The numbers vary, depending on what criteria is used. One of the reasons I did not use data from 2013 on is that many of the court cases have not all had the chance to matriculate through the system yet and thus, not all of the information has been vetted properly.

A quick confession.

I despise anything that reads like academia. I'm not saying all academia is bad, or that professors are bad, or that universities are bad. I'm just saying that when I read an academic textbook or paper, I want to hurl myself through a window.

Thus, the following section is not cited in the way an academic would. I opted not to use the APA format, or any other format, to cite my sources because I am not here to amaze you with my awesome abilities to use other people's work to make my point. I wrote this section to discuss Mass Shootings in the United States, and have provided loose references in the text. My reason for this is that I want you to know where I got my information, so that you can be assured of where it comes from.

Another quick note before we get started.

Killers are not included in the death toll for any of the incidents where they died at the scene. The way I see it, they don't deserve to be counted next to the people they murdered.

1. Date: June 29, 1984

Location: Ianni's Club in Dallas, TX

Suspect: Abdelkrim Belachheb, 39

Killed/Injured: 6 killed, 1 injured

Weapon Used in Incident: Smith & Wesson 9mm pistol

Weapon Purchased Legally? Unknown. A New York Times article dated June 30, 1984, states that the gun used was "his."

Summary: Belachheb, an unemployed Moroccan immigrant, was rejected by a dance partner and went out to his car to retrieve his weapon. He returned to the club, shot her, and gunned down five others.

Event Ended By: He fled the scene and was arrested by Dallas PD.

2. Date: July 18, 1984

Location: McDonald's Restaurant in San Ysidro, CA

Suspect: James Oliver Huberty, 41

Killed/Injured: 21 killed, 19 injured

Weapon Used in Incident: Browning P-35 9mm pistol, Winchester 1200 pump-action 12-gauge shotgun, Israeli Military Industries 9mm Model A Carbine (Uzi)

Weapon Purchased Legally? Yes.

Summary: Huberty, an unemployed welder, entered a McDonald's and proceeded to murder the people inside. The event lasted seventy-seven minutes as police arrived and contained the scene.

Event Ended By: A SWAT sniper named **CHUCK FOSTER**. According to the San Diego Police museum, Foster made the shot from the roof of a nearby post office, hitting Huberty through a window. One shot. One kill.

3. Date: August 20, 1986

Location: Edmond Post Office in Edmond, OK

Suspect: Patrick Sherrill, 44

Killed/Injured: 14 killed, 6 injured

Weapon Used in Incident: Two .45 pistols, a .22 pistol

Weapon Purchased Legally? Yes

Summary: Sherill was a former marine and part-time post office employee at the Edmond location. He had been disciplined the day before the event and returned at 0700 hours on the day of the massacre, carrying weapons and ammo with him. Some reports say he barred the doors to prevent escape, while others say he simply went from desk to desk, shooting anyone he saw. This is the incident that is commonly credited with coining the phrase, "going postal."

Event Ended By: Sherill self-inflicted at the scene.

5. Date: January 17, 1989

Location: Cleveland Elementary School Schoolyard. Stockton, CA

Suspect: Patrick Purdy, 24

Killed/Injured: 5 killed, 30 injured

Weapon Used in Incident: Chinese-made AK-47-type assault rifle, Taurus 9mm pistol.

Weapon Purchased Legally? Yes.

Summary: In a Deseret News article published on January 18, 1989, Patrick Purdy is described as a troubled drifter who had been in trouble numerous times with the law. On the date of the shooting, Purdy parked his van behind the Cleveland Elementary School and lit it on fire. He then walked over to the playground and took cover behind a building before aiming his rifle at a group of children playing, and shooting at them. He killed five children and wounded thirty others. All of the murdered children, and most of the injured ones, were of Southeast Asian descent. In a Prescott Courier article dated January 19, 1989, it was reported that Purdy was said to hate Vietnamese people and blamed them for stealing American jobs.

Event Ended By: Purdy self-inflicted at the scene.

6. Date: September 14, 1989

Location: Standard Gravure Corporation, Louisville, KY

Suspect: Joseph Wesbecker, 47

Killed/Injured: 8 killed, 12 injured

Weapon Used in Incident: Chinese-made AK-47-type assault rifle, two INTRATEC MAC-11 assault pistols, SIG SAUER 9mm pistol, and a .38 revolver.

Weapon Purchased Legally? Yes.

Summary: Wesbecker had been placed on leave from his printing job at Standard Gravure on mental disability. According to an article in the Deseret News, published September 17, 1989, Wesbecker possibly received notice that his disability checks were being cancelled, prior to the event. He entered the location and began killing secretaries, supervisors, and employees.

Event Ended By: Wesbecker self-inflicted at the scene.

7. Date: June 18, 1990

Location: General Motors Acceptance Corporation Office, Jacksonville, FL

Suspect: James Edward Pough, 42

Killed/Injured: 9 killed, 4 injured

Weapon Used in Incident: Universal M1 .30-caliber assault rifle, and a .38 revolver

Weapon Purchased Legally? No. The Violence Policy Center lists the weapons in this incident as legally purchased, but they are incorrect. Pough was a convicted felon who had previously been arrested for murder. According to a New York Times article dated June 19, 1990, he lied on his application to purchase the handgun.

Summary: The motives behind Pough's violence that day are not clear, although it is speculated that he blamed General Motors for the recent repossession of his car. He had no definitive connection to the location of his crime or the victims he shot. He is described as systematically moving through the office, firing at people as they hid under desks.

Event Ended By: Pough self-inflicted at the scene.

8. Date: October 16, 1991

Location: Luby's Cafeteria in Killeen, TX

Suspect: George Hennard, 35

Killed/Injured: 23 killed, 20 injured

Weapon Used in Incident: GLOCK 17 9mm pistol, and Ruger P89 pistol

Weapon Purchased Legally? Yes.

Summary: According to a New York Times article published October 18, 1991, Hennard was an unemployed and difficult loner who appeared strangely friendly on the morning of 16th. He smashed his truck through the front window of a local diner and started killing the people inside. At the time the New York City Crime Commission published its findings, Hennard's motive for his actions that day still could not be determined.

Event Ended By: According to a People magazine article dated November 4, 1991, Hennard was shot four times by responding officers. He then fled into the bathroom and self-inflicted.

9. Date: July 1, 1993

Location: Pettit & Martin Law Firm, San Francisco, CA

Suspect: Gian Luigi Ferri, 55

Killed/Injured: 8 killed, 6 injured

Weapon Used in Incident: Two INTRATEC TEC-DC9 pistols, and Colt .45 pistol

Weapon Purchased Legally? Yes.

Summary: A mentally unstable Ferri entered a law firm and began firing. During his onslaught, he killed attorneys, secretaries, and people involved in various law suits. Investigators later found a rambling hand-written note that blamed multiple factors for his problems, including being poisoned by MSG (monosodium glutamate).

Event Ended By: Ferri self-inflicted at the scene.

10. Date: December 7, 1993

Location: Long Island Railroad, Long Island, NY

Suspect: Colin Ferguson, 35

Killed/Injured: 6 killed, 19 injured

Weapon Used in Incident: Ruger P89 9mm pistol

Weapon Purchased Legally? Yes.

Summary: Ferguson boarded a train heading toward the Merillon Avenue Station aboard a crowded car, when he drew his handgun and began firing at the passengers all around him. He emptied his magazine, reloaded, and continued firing.

Event Ended By: A New York Times article published on December 9, 1993, credits **MICHAEL O'CONNOR, MARK McENTEE**, and **KEVIN BLUM** as being the three men who charged Ferguson and ended the rampage. Unbeknownst to them, he had more than one hundred additional rounds in a canvas bag that he likely would have kept using if they had not found the courage to intervene.

A NY Daily News article published on December 17, 2013, provides more specific details of **KEVIN BLUM'S** actions that day. The then forty-two-year old stockbroker watched Ferguson shoot a woman at point blank range directly in front of him and he picked up his briefcase and charged, knocking the gunman down so that everyone could pile on top of him. Ferguson was then handcuffed by an off-duty Long Island Rail Road police officer named **ANDREW RODERICK,** who was in the area to pick up his wife.

11. Date: June 20, 1994

Location: Fairchild Air Force Base, WA

Suspect: Dean Allen Mellberg, 20

Killed/Injured: 5 killed, 23 injured

Weapon Used in Incident: Chinese-made Mak-90 assault rifle

Weapon Purchased Legally? Yes.

Summary: Mellberg was released from the Air Force involuntarily and returned weeks later to exact vengeance on the people he thought responsible. He targeted doctors and others inside the hospital and as he chased more intended victims outside, intending to gun them down.

Event Ended By: As Mellberg left the hospital, he was confronted by Senior Airman **ANDREW BROWN.** According to the OSI Official report and Spokane County Sheriff's Office report, **BROWN**, a military policeman on bicycle patrol that day, was responding to the scene in time to see Mellberg come running out. From seventy yards out, **ANDY BROWN** shot Mellberg twice and put an end to the massacre.

12. Date: November 22, 1994

Location: DC Police Headquarters, Washington DC

Suspect: Bennie L. Lawson Jr., 25

Killed/Injured: 3 killed, 2 injured

Weapon Used in Incident: Cobray M-11 assault pistol

Weapon Purchased Legally? No.

Summary: Lawson had been interviewed by DC Homicide several days before the incident and told he was going to be charged. He returned to the station and asked for directions to Homicide, but was taken instead to the Cold Case Squad office. He encountered three FBI agents and a DC sergeant inside, and opened fire. The sergeant and two of the FBI agents were murdered, and a third agent was shot five times but survived.

Event Ended By: According to an article in D.C. Crime Stories, November 22, 2013, Agent **MARTHA DIXON MARTINEZ** shot Lawson before he could shoot her. Her wound caused her to drop her gun and Lawson picked it up, shot her in the head, and then shot himself.

According to the FBI's Hall of Honor, **MARTINEZ** was the first female agent in her Knoxville field office to be certified as a SWAT member. She is one of two female FBI agents to have been killed in the line of duty.

13. Date: April 4, 1995

Location: Walter Rossler Company, Corpus Christi, TX

Suspect: James Simpson, 28

Killed/Injured: 5 killed

Weapon Used in Incident: Ruger 9mm pistol and .32 revolver

Weapon Purchased Legally? Yes.

Summary: Simpson was a former employee at the Walter Rossler Company and he entered the business and killed the owner, the owner's wife, and three others. According to a New York Times article published April 4, 1995, several people escaped the building through the rear entrance. The Chief of Police was quoted in the article as saying that everyone Simpson encountered, he killed.

Event Ended By: Simpson self-inflicted at the scene.

14. Date: September 15, 1997

Location: R.E. Phelon Company, Aiken, SC

Suspect: Hastings Arthur Wise, 43

Killed/Injured: 4 killed, 3 injured

Weapon Used in Incident: 9mm pistol

Weapon Purchased Legally? No. Wise was a convicted felon and could not have obtained the handgun legally.

Summary: Wise was an ex-employee at R.E. Phelon. He returned with a handgun and began executing employees before swallowing insecticide.

Event Ended By: The insecticide did not kill him, as intended. It only made him violently ill, incapacitating him until police arrived to arrest him.

15. Date: October 1, 1997

Location: Pearl High School, Pearl, MS

Suspect: Luke Woodham, 16

Killed/Injured: 3 killed, 7 injured

Weapon Used in Incident: Marlin Model 336 .30-30-caliber rifle, Knife.

Weapon Purchased Legally? Woodham stole the rifle from his older brother.

Summary: Luke Woodham stabbed his mother to death at their residence and then drove her car to school. Upon entering the school, he murdered three classmates and injured seven more.

Event Ended By: The assault was stopped by assistant principal **JOEL MYRICK**, who retrieved a .45 caliber semi-automatic pistol from his truck. **MYRICK** was a National Guard combat unit commander, and he located Woodham in the parking lot and was able to detain him until police arrived.

Unfortunately, **MYRICK'S** actions that day have become a lightning rod for conspiracy theorists who insist the media is purposely not reporting the effectiveness of armed civilians preventing tragedies, as well as people on both sides of the gun control issue. Regardless of how people choose to exploit what he did for their own selfish purposes, **JOEL MYRICK** deserves recognition for the lives he saved that day by taking action.

16. Date: December 1, 1997

Location: Heath High School, West Paducah, KY

Suspect: Michael Carneal, 14

Killed/Injured: 3 killed, 5 injured

Weapon Used in Incident: Ruger .22 pistol

Weapon Purchased Legally? No. He stole a large cache of weapons from a family friend, including the one he used in the murders.

Summary: According to a CNN article dated December 1, 1997, Carneal went to the school lobby in the morning where a prayer group was gathered.

Event Ended By: Carneal shot multiple people before dropping his weapon and telling the school principal he was sorry.

17. Date: December 18, 1997

Location: Caltrans Maintenance Yard, Orange, CA

Suspect: Arturo Reyes Torres, 41

Killed/Injured: 4 killed, 2 injured

Weapon Used in Incident: Chinese-made AK-47-type assault rifle

Weapon Purchased Legally? Yes.

Summary: Torres had been fired from his job for stealing. He returned to the location and began shooting people with an AK-47.

Event Ended By: According to an LA Times article dated December 19, 1997, responding officers exchanged gunfire with Torres, before he fled in a vehicle. They located him and a second firefight ensued where officers engaged this deadly maniac armed with an AK-47 and defeated him.

18. Date: March 6, 1998

Location: Connecticut State Lottery Headquarters, Newington, CT

Suspect: Matthew Beck, 35

Killed/Injured: 4 killed, none injured

Weapon Used in Incident: 9mm Glock pistol

Weapon Purchased Legally? Yes

Summary: A disgruntled State Lottery employee who had been recently passed over for promotion returned to work on March 6, 1998, and began executing his supervisors.

Event Ended By: According to a NY Times article dated, March 7, 1998, Beck murdered three bosses inside the Lottery building and chased a fourth one outside into the parking lot. Just as he was about to shoot, Newington detectives arrived and began making their approach. Beck saw them, killed the man he was chasing, then raised the gun and self-inflicted.

19. Date: March 24, 1998

Location: Westside Middle School, Jonesboro, AR

Suspect: Andrew Golden, 11, and Mitchell Johnson, 13

Killed/Injured: 5 killed, 10 injured

Weapon Used in Incident: Remington Model 742 .30-06 rifle, Universal .30 M1 Carbine replica, Davis Industries .38 two-shot derringer, Double Deuce Buddie .22 two-shot derringer, Charter Arms .38 revolver, Star .380 pistol, FIE .380 pistol, Ruger Security Six .357 revolver

Smith & Wesson .38 revolver

Weapon Purchased Legally? No. The weapons were stolen.

Summary: On the date of the incident, both suspects stole a van from the Johnson family and drove to Golden's grandparents' house to steal the weapons they would use in the assault. The pair then drove to Westside Middle School, where Golden walked in and pulled the fire alarm. He ran outside to meet Johnson and they armed themselves. As multiple students and teachers came running out of the school, both boys opened fire. They killed four children and one teacher and wounded multiple others.

Event Ended By: Both boys fled into the woods before they were captured by police. In what is truly the most astonishing outcome to any of these cases, both Golden and Johnson spent less than ten years a piece in juvenile prison before being released on their twenty-first birthdays.

Johnson, who was thirteen years old at the time of the murders, claimed that eleven year old Golden had come up with the plan, and thought they were only going to frighten bullies in the school. He did seven years for the murder of four children and one teacher. Golden did a grand total of nine.

According to an Arkansas Times article on December 11, 2008, Andrew Golden changed his name to Drew Douglas Grant and attempted to acquire a concealed handgun permit. The permit was denied by the Sharp County sheriff after it was discovered Grant and Golden were the same person.

Mitchell Johnson continuously ran into trouble with police since being released from juvenile prison in 2005. According to a USA Today article published January 23, 2009, Johnson was arrested three times in three years for offenses that included theft, fraud, and carrying a handgun. As of this writing, he is still in prison.

20. Date: May 21, 1998

Location: Thurston High School, Springfield, OR

Suspect: Kipland Philip "Kip" Kinkel, 15

Killed/Injured: 4 killed, 25 injured

Weapon Used in Incident: Glock 9mm pistol, Ruger .22 rifle, and a Ruger .22 pistol

Weapon Purchased Legally? Unclear. VCP lists the weapons used in this incident as being legally purchased, but Kinkel's father purchased the Glock and rifle for him. I don't know enough about 1980's gun laws in Oregon to know if that was permissible or not. It has been established that Kinkel purchased a .32 Beretta from one of his friends at school who had stolen it from his own father.

Summary: According to a PBS Frontline chronological profile of Kip Kinkel, he arrived at school at 0800, May 20, 1998, with $110 cash to purchase the Beretta. He subsequently placed the gun in his locker. The owner of the Beretta called the police to report that he thought his son had taken the gun. Police responded to the school and subsequently learned that Kinkel had purchased the gun and it was still in the school. Both Kinkel, and the boy who sold it to him, were arrested and suspended, with the understanding they would be expelled. Kinkel was released from the police station to his father. The two of them returned home to wait for Mrs. Kinkel to get home and tell her the bad news.

At 1500 hours, Kinkel walked up behind his father in the kitchen and shot him through the back of the head with the .22 rifle. If you recall, Mr. Kinkel had bought his son the rifle with the understanding it would only be used under his supervision.

At approximately 1830 hours, Mrs. Kinkel returned home, still unaware of the earlier incident. Kinkel met his mother in the garage, said that he loved her, and shot her to death.

The next morning, Kinkel armed himself with three guns and a hunting knife. He drove his mother's car to the school and walked in, killed two people, and injured multiple others.

Event Ended By: A NY Times article dated May 23, 1998, writes that seventeen-year-old **JACOB RYDER** was sitting in the school cafeteria when Kip Kinkel began shooting. **RYDER** took a round to the chest, the bullet piercing his right lung, but got to his feet and immediately charged Kinkel. **RYDER**, a wrestler and hunter, got Kinkel on the ground and "pounded him." Kinkel managed to grab the 9mm and fired it at **RYDER**, shooting him in the hand. At this point, three other students jumped in, and together, they ended the rampage. Those students' names are **JOSHUA RYDER, DAVID URE,** and **ADAM WALBERGER**.

I'm not normally one to pass judgment on other cops unless I'm there to see what happened, but since we're all friends here, I'll say this: If an armed psychopath just burst into a school and started shooting kids with multiple weapons, I'd think you'd want to search him pretty thoroughly.

Well.

Remember that hunting knife I told you Kinkel had? He taped it to his leg, and the arresting officer missed it. The detective who took custody of Kinkel from that officer missed it. Then another detective showed up to do the transport and he missed it too.

Kinkel, while cuffed at the station, pulled the knife out and charged the detective, trying to achieve suicide by cop. Two detectives were able to pepper spray Kinkel and finally disarm him. A later search would reveal that Kinkel had two bullets taped to his chest, one for each of his pistols in case he ran empty and needed one last bullet to self-inflict.

Kinkel was sentenced to 111 years in prison and is still incarcerated.

Let me take off my researcher hat for a moment and step back in here so we can talk this one out. I'm honestly not slamming the officers involved in this arrest, and I'm sure if they were here, they would be able to describe the mass chaos of the scene when they showed up. At the time, they were dealing with dead bodies, injured students, an enraged crowd, and a mass murderer. Friends, that is a full plate no matter who you are or where you work.

However, what stands out in my mind is that Kinkel was able to pull the knife and charge with it while handcuffed. It doesn't take a rocket scientist to realize they cuffed a crazed mass murderer in front. That's inexcusable. Miss the knife at the scene because you're too busy trying to keep your suspect from getting pummeled to death, okay, I'll give you that one. Your hands are shaking, you're distracted, you're horrified by the scene, I get it. But miss the knife when you are handed the bad guy and do a secondary search? Transport him cuffed in front? You lost me there.

There are multiple lessons to be learned from every incident listed here, but this one has special importance to every single one of us. I don't care how crazy things are, how freaked out you get, or how much of a rush you are in. This is basic police academy tactics. Cuff your suspects in the back and then conduct your search. If they have one weapon, they have two. If they have two weapons, they have four hundred.

All right, let's get back to work.

21. Date: April 20, 1999

Location: Columbine High School, Littleton, CO

Suspect: Eric Harris, 18, and Dylan Klebold, 17

Killed/Injured: 13 killed, 23 injured

Weapon Used in Incident: Savage Springfield 67H 12-gauge shotgun, Savage Stevens 311D 12-gauge shotgun, Hi-Point 995 9mm rifle, INTRATEC TEC-DC9 9mm pistol, and pipe bombs

Weapon Purchased Legally? No.

Summary: For forty-nine minutes, Eric Harris and Dylan Klebold assaulted the students and faculty of Columbine High School with pipe bombs and heavy weaponry. The following information is based on a CNN narrative timeline of the events of that day as well as accounts provided by the NYCCC and VCP.

At approximately 1119 hours, police were dispatched to an explosion three miles away from Columbine High School. The explosion was caused by two backpacks Harris and Klebold had rigged to a timer to blow up and divert police so they could begin their assault on the high school.

Both suspects then entered the school parking lot on foot and began shooting and killing students.

At 1124 hours, a police deputy arrives on scene and engages Eric Harris in a brief gunfight. Neither of them is hit, and Harris runs into the high school. The deputy remains outside. Both suspects continue their rampage inside the school, unhindered.

At 1128 hours, students advise police officers outside of the school that Harris and Klebold are killing people inside. The officers remain outside.

By 1132 hours, assisting officers are responding to the scene. The officers remain outside.

Explosions can be heard from inside the school as Harris and Klebold continue to toss pipe bombs inside the building. Reports of the explosions are radioed in to dispatch by police on scene. They are still outside.

It is now 1146 hours, and the suspects set off a bomb inside the cafeteria. There are students in the immediate area because school surveillance video shows them fleeing through the side door of the cafeteria while it burns. All of this is reported by officers on scene, who remain outside.

At 1152 hours, the Jefferson County Undersheriff arrives and authorizes the recently-arrived SWAT to make entry. They make their first approach approximately ten minutes later.

Event Ended By: At approximately 1208 hours, after a rampage that lasted approximately forty-nine minutes and claimed the lives of thirteen people and wounded twenty-three others, Dylan Harris and Eric Klebold killed themselves in the library.

The lasting effects of the Columbine shooting on both the national psyche and law enforcement are incalculable. In those forty-nine minutes, our tactics, techniques, and determination to rapidly respond to active shooter events changed forever.

22. Date: May 20, 1999

Location: Heritage High School, Conyers, GA

Suspect: Thomas (TJ) Solomon, Jr, 15

Killed/Injured: 6 injured

Weapon Used in Incident: .22 rifle, .357 Magnum revolver

Weapon Purchased Legally? No. The weapons were stolen from his father.

Summary: Exactly one month after Columbine, another school shooting. In a December 19, 2012, news article by Atlanta's 11 Alive, it was the first of several copycat shootings that would take place in the wake of Columbine. In this instance, a 15 year old stole his father's guns and opened fire on students gathered in the commons area of his high school.

Event Ended By: A sixty-year-old Assistant Principal named **CECIL BRINKLEY**, on his last day of school before retirement, confronted Solomon and disarmed him. According to an article in the Eugene Register-Guard published May 22, 1999, **BRINKLEY** took a shortcut in the hallways that allowed him to head off Solomon. The suspect turned and aimed the .357 at him, and **BRINKLEY** talked him down and disarmed him.

23. Date: July 29, 1999

Location: Various Atlanta Brokerage Offices, Atlanta, GA

Suspect: Mark O. Barton, 44

Killed/Injured: 12 killed, 13 injured

Weapon Used in Incident: Glock Model 17 9mm pistol, Colt 1911A1 .45 pistol

Weapon Purchased Legally? Yes.

Summary: According to a CNN article dated July 30, 1999, Barton was a trained chemist who later turned to day-trading to earn his living. Apparently he wasn't very good at it, because he'd recently lost over one hundred thousand dollars in a short period of time.

Six years prior to the murders that day, Barton's wife and mother-in-law were found beaten to death at a campsite. Barton was a suspect in those crimes, but never indicted.

He later remarried and fathered two children, an eleven-year-old boy and a seven-year-old girl. Then he killed them, beating both of his children and his wife to death with a hammer.

At approximately 1500 hours, Barton walked into Momentum Securities and killed four people. He then walked across the street to All-Tech and killed five more people.

Event Ended By: Barton fled the scene and police searched for him for five hours before he self-inflicted.

24. Date: September 15, 1999

Location: Wedgewood Baptist Church, Fort Worth, TX

Suspect: Larry Gene Ashbrook, 47

Killed/Injured: 7 killed, 7 injured

Weapon Used in Incident: Ruger P85 9mm pistol, and .380 pistol

Weapon Purchased Legally? Yes.

Summary: Larry Ashbrook was a psychologically disturbed person who murdered seven people and wounded seven others during a Christian rock concert. According to a Time Magazine report dated September 20, 1999, there was little to no connection between the shooter and the church or his victims.

Event Ended By: Ashbrook sat down in one of the church pews and self-inflicted.

25. Date: November 2, 1999

Location: Xerox Office Building, Honolulu, HI

Suspect: Byran Uyesugi, 40

Killed/Injured: 7 killed, none injured

Weapon Used in Incident: Glock Model 17 9mm pistol

Weapon Purchased Legally? Yes.

Summary: According to a NY Times article from November 3, 1999, Uyesugi was a Xerox employee who walked into the office building and began shooting. His victims were all between the ages of 33 and 58, and were all male.

Event Ended By: Uyesugi fled the scene in a van and drove to the Hawaii Nature Center. Police responded and successfully negotiated his surrender. He was subsequently sentenced to life in prison.

26. Date: December 6, 1999

Location: Fort Gibson Middle School, Fort Gibson, OK

Suspect: Seth Trickey, 13

Killed/Injured: None killed, 4 injured

Weapon Used in Incident: Taurus 9mm pistol

Weapon Purchased Legally? No. Stolen from his father.

Summary: By all accounts, Seth Trickey was not a person anyone expected to be on this list. According to a December 14, 1999, article in the Chicago Tribune, Trickey was a straight-A student, nice kid, who people described as shy and sweet. And yet, on December 6, 1999, he went to school with his father's stolen gun and ammo and shot four people. Luckily, no one was killed. The injured people appeared to be randomly hit by stray rounds.

Event Ended By: After emptying his magazine, Trickey dropped the empty gun and was grabbed by science teacher **RONNIE HOLUBY**. **HOLUBY** pinned Trickey's arms down and held him against a brick wall until police arrived. According to a 2005 article in TulsaWorld, Trickey was released from prison at the age of eighteen. He never gave a clear reason for the shooting, other than to say he was obsessed with the military, under pressure from his family and had been infatuated with Columbine.

27. Date: March 20, 2000

Location: Mi-T-Fine Car Wash, Irving, TX

Suspect: Robert Wayne Harris, 28

Killed/Injured: 5 killed, 1 injured

Weapon Used in Incident: 9mm pistol

Weapon Purchased Legally? Illegal. Borrowed the pistol from a friend.

Summary: According to an ABC news article dated September 25, 2001, and an Associated Press article that appeared September 20, 2012, in the Dallas Morning News after Harris was executed, he was a convicted burglar who spent eight years in prison and got a job at the Mi-T-Fine car wash upon being released. He worked there for ten months before being fired and arrested for exposing himself to a female customer while leaving the restroom door open.

He arrived at the car wash the following Monday before it opened and found three employees inside. He removed $4k from the safe and made the employees lie face down on the office floor, then shot each of them in the back of the head. Three more employees arrived for work and Harris made each of them lie face down in the lobby and he shot them in the back of head too, although one survived. A final employee arrived for work, saw Harris and the bloody scene, and ran across the street to a local donut shop to call police.

Event Ended By: While the employee was on the phone with 911, he saw Harris coming into the shop. Harris picked up the phone, told the dispatcher who he was, made a flimsy excuse about coming to work and finding all the blood, and then ran off.

Police found him the next day hiding in a friend's house.

And, just to mention the benefits of always doing a full a complete interview with everyone you arrest, especially asking them, "Is there anything else you want to tell me about?" the day after Harris was arrested, he took police to the location of another dead body. He'd killed a 37-year-old woman approximately four months prior to the carwash incident, and left her hidden in a weeded area.

28. Date: April 24, 2000

Location: National Zoo, Washington, DC

Suspect: Antoine Jones, 16

Killed/Injured: None killed, 7 injured

Weapon Used in Incident: 9mm pistol

Weapon Purchased Legally? Illegal.

Summary: According to a NY Times article dated April 26, 2000, it is a long standing tradition for African American families to gather at the zoo in Woodley Park on the Monday after Easter. This shooting occurred when Jones fired at a crowd of people exiting from the zoo's west gate. The victims were all children.

Event Ended By: Antoine Jones was arrested the next day. He was subsequently tried as an adult, and according to a Chicago Tribune article dated March 17, 2001, he plead guilty and received a twenty-five year sentence.

A Baltimore Sun article dated April 26, 2000, says that the zoo's director wanted to make sure a similar event never happened again. Sadly, it did. On April 21, 2014, a 14-year-old was arrested for attempted murder when he shot into a crowd gathered at the zoo for the same annual event and injured two people.

29. Date: December 26, 2000

Location: Edgewater Technology office, Wakefield, MA

Suspect: Michael McDermott, 42

Killed/Injured: 7 killed, none injured

Weapon Used in Incident: AK-47 assault rifle, 12-gauge shotgun, and .32 pistol

Weapon Purchased Legally? Yes.

Summary: McDermott was employed at Edgewater in application support and had recently been experiencing tax trouble. According to a NY Times article published December 27, 2000, the IRS had instructed Edgewater Tech to begin garnishing McDermott's wages in order to repay his debt. McDermott arrived at work the day after Christmas at 0900 and spoke to his co-workers as usual. At approximately 1100 hours, he picked up his weapons and began shooting for five to ten minutes. Witnesses stated the majority of people he killed had no connection to him.

Event Ended By: After the five minute rampage, McDermott sat down in the reception area and waited for authorities. He was arrested and later sentenced to multiple life sentences.

30. Date: February 5, 2001

Location: Navistar International Corporation, Melrose Park, IL

Suspect: William Baker, 66

Killed/Injured: 5 killed, 4 injured

Weapon Used in Incident: SKS 1954R rifle, Remington 12-gauge shotgun, Winchester .30 rifle, and .38 revolver

Weapon Purchased Legally? No. Baker was a convicted felon and not allowed to purchase firearms, however he was able to renew his FOID card and purchase the weapons at a local gun store.

Summary: An ABC News article dated February 6, 2001, reveals that Baker had been convicted for attempting to steal from Navistar and on the day of the killings, he was supposed to begin serving his federal prison sentence. Baker pulled a gun on a security guard and forced his way into the building where he then removed the rest of his weapons from inside a gold bag and began shooting.

Event Ended By: Baker self-inflicted at the scene.

31. Date: March 5, 2001

Location: Santee High School, Santana, CA

Suspect: Charles Andrew Williams, 15

Killed/Injured: 2 killed, 13 injured

Weapon Used in Incident: .22 Arminius eight-shot revolver

Weapon Purchased Legally? No. Stolen from father

Summary: In an ABC News article dated October 10 (no year given) detailing the events of the day and an interview Williams gave with Diane Sawyer, it describes that Williams entered his school's bathroom and loaded his father's stolen gun. When Williams exited the bathroom, he was smiling and shooting. Williams subsequently retreated back into the bathroom.

Event Ended By: According to SFGate.com, Deputy **ALI PEREZ** was inside the school when the rampage began, giving a lecture to a class. He immediately responded toward the sound of gunfire. Astonishingly enough, a second police officer named **BOB CLARK** was in the school off-duty to register his daughter, and he joined **PEREZ** in containing the shooter inside the bathroom. Three responding officers arrived and together, the group of them stormed the bathroom and took Williams into custody.

Williams was sentenced fifty years to life and is still in prison. He has since given interviews to Diane Sawyer and PBS News Hour about his life and thoughts on mass shooters.

32. Date: November 21, 2004

Location: Hunting Camp, Meteor, WI

Suspect: Chai Vang, 36

Killed/Injured: 6 killed, 3 injured

Weapon Used in Incident: SKS 7.62mm assault rifle

Weapon Purchased Legally? Yes.

Summary: Vang was hunting in Wisconsin and got lost in the woods. He wound up on private property, found an unused tree stand, and climbed up to wait for a deer. Instead, he was seen by members of a hunting party in the area who told him to leave. Vang climbed down and opened fire, killing and injuring multiple people.

Event Ended By: According to a FoxNews report dated November 22, 2004, one of the members of the hunting party managed to write down Vang's hunter ID number. Vang fled into the woods and was picked up by two other hunters who were aware of the shootings. They took him directly to a nearby game warden who arrested him. Vang would later claim he'd killed the men in racial self-defense, but investigators found just one gun among the group of men he'd shot. The same article states that Vang had previously been arrested for threatening his wife with a gun. Vang was convicted and received six life sentences.

33. Date: January 30, 2006

Location: Santa Barbara Postal Processing and Distribution Center, Goleta, CA

Suspect: Jennifer San Marco, 44

Killed/Injured: 7 killed, none injured

Weapon Used in Incident: Smith & Wesson 915 9mm handgun

Weapon Purchased Legally? Yes.

Summary: Three years after leaving the postal service for psychological reasons, San Marco returned with a gun. She shot two people in the parking lot and four inside the building. No definitive motive was ever discovered, however, investigators recovered writings at the suspect's home that described a complicated conspiracy involving the postal center and other agencies.

Event Ended By: San Marco self-inflicted at the scene.

34. Date: April 16, 2007

Location: Virginia Polytechnic Institute and State University, Blacksburg, VA

Suspect: Seung-Hui Cho, 23

Killed/Injured: 32 killed, 17 injured

Weapon Used in Incident: GLOCK 19 9mm pistol and Walther P22 .22-caliber pistol.

Weapon Purchased Legally? Yes.

Summary: See Chapter 3 for details

Event Ended By: Self-inflicted at the scene

35. Date: December 5, 2007

Location: Westroads Mall, Omaha, NE

Suspect: Robert Hawkins, 19

Killed/Injured: 8 killed, 5 injured

Weapon Used in Incident: WASR-10 assault rifle

Weapon Purchased Legally? No. Stolen from his step-father.

Summary: According to a FoxNews report dated December 6, 2007, Robert Hawkins left a suicide note in his car when he parked it at the Westroads Mall that said he was "going out in style" and "going to be famous." At 1400 hours on a Wednesday, he entered the mall and walked up to the third floor balcony where he aimed his weapon and began shooting at the people beneath.

Event Ended By: Police arrived within six minutes, but by then, eight people were dead and another fifteen were injured. Hawkins self-inflicted at the scene.

36. Date: February 14, 2008

Location: Northern Illinois University, DeKalb, IL

Suspect: Steven Phillip Kazmierczak, 27

Killed/Injured: 5 killed, 21 injured

Weapon Used in Incident: SIG SAUER Kurz 9mm pistol, Hi-Point CF380 .380 caliber pistol, GLOCK 19 9mm pistol, and Remington Sportsman 48 12-gauge shotgun.

Weapon Purchased Legally? Yes.

Summary: According to an article published in the LA Times, March 22, 2010, Kazmierczak had been a standout student at Northern Illinois University from 2002 to 2006. He graduated with a 3.88 GPA and was considered the "golden boy" of their sociology department. But things were not always so easy. A CBSNews report dated February 16, 2008, details how Kazmierczak had been committed by his parents while he was in high school. He then entered the Army, but was released for lying about his mental health issues.

Upon graduating college, he became a corrections officer at the Rockville Correctional Facility, which lasted for a year until he stopped showing up for work. He then re-enrolled in the college as an undergraduate. On Valentine's Day, 2008, he kicked a door open to the Cole Hall auditorium and began shooting.

Event Ended By: Self-inflicted at the scene.

37. Date: March 29, 2009

Location: Carthage nursing home shooting, Carthage, NC

Suspect: Robert Stewart, 45

Killed/Injured: 8 killed, 2 injured

Weapon Used in Incident: 12-gauge Winchester 1300 shotgun, .357 Magnum revolver, .22 Magnum pistol

Weapon Purchased Legally? Unknown

Summary: Stewart, an unemployed and disabled painter, went to his estranged wife's place of work and went on a rampage, killing eight people. His wife was not harmed.

Event Ended By: According to NBC News, March 30, 2009, the event was ended by a single police officer. **JUSTIN GARNER** responded to the scene within one minute and confronted Stewart. A firefight ensued where **GARNER** was hit three times in the leg, but he placed one round in the center of Stewart's chest and ended the fight. Stewart survived being shot but is now serving life in prison. During the investigation, police found the body of US Coast Guard veteran and nurse **JERRY AVANT JR.** According to a WRAL article dated April 2, 2009, **AVANT** shielded his elderly patients from Stewart's bullets. He perished after being shot two dozen times.

38. Date: April 3, 2009

Location: American Civic Association Immigration Center, Binghamton, NY

Suspect: Jiverly Wong, 41

Killed/Injured: 13 killed, 4 injured

Weapon Used in Incident: Beretta .45-caliber pistol, Beretta 9mm pistol

Weapon Purchased Legally? Yes.

Summary: On the night of the incident, Wong backed his car up to the Civic Association's rear exit and blocked it off. He then entered through the front and began firing at the people in the reception area, then going into a classroom and shooting the teacher and students inside. Wong had been an English student at the center for a brief period of time prior to the shootings, although according to the NY Times in an article dated April 11, 2009, he had immigrated to the US back in 1990. No clear motive was ever established for why Wong returned to the center or why he targeted the people there.

Event Ended By: Wong self-inflicted at the scene.

39. Date: November 5, 2009

Location: Fort Hood, Fort Hood, TX

Suspect: Nidal Malik Hasan, 39

Killed/Injured: 13 killed, 32 injured

Weapon Used in Incident: FN Herstal 5.7 Tactical Pistol

Weapon Purchased Legally? Yes.

Summary: Hassan, an army psychologist, entered the Fort Hood medical processing center and began firing on the people within. According to a NY Daily News article dated August 7, 2013, Hasan said he committed the crime to protect the Taliban in Afghanistan. The article claims Hasan shouted "Allahu akbar," which means "God is great" in Arabic, before the murders.

The warriors at Fort Hood were unarmed, but they did not go without a fight.

According to the Killeen Daily Herald, January 23, 2014, Specialist **FREDERICK GREENE** was shot two dozen times while charging Hasan.

According to CNN, August 9, 2013, Captain **JOHN GAFFNEY** raced toward Hasan with a folding chair before he was gunned down. The same article details how Spec. **LOGAN BARNETT** was throwing a folding table at Hasan when Hasan turned and shot him in the head. **BARNETT** shielded two escaping officers with his own body before eventually crawling out of the room.

Event Ended By: Initial reports claimed that base civilian police Sergeant **KIMBERLY MUNLEY** arrived on scene as Hasan came out of the processing center. According to NY Daily News,

November 7, 2009, **MUNLEY** said she exchanged fire with Hasan, getting hit several times in the legs before putting him down.

It was then reported by multiple sources, including the NY Times, November 12, 2009, that Hasan was actually shot by Sgt. **MARK TODD**. **TODD** would later provide a detailed account of how he kicked Hasan's weapon away and placed him in custody.

Regardless of whose bullets put Hasan down, both officers should be credited with getting there in time to end the threat. As for Hasan, he has been sentenced to death and is currently sitting in prison. Specifically, sitting, because he was paralyzed that day from the waist down.

40. Date: August 3, 2010

Location: Hartford Beer Distributor, Manchester, CT

Suspect: Omar Thornton, 34

Killed/Injured: 8 killed, 2 injured

Weapon Used in Incident: Two Ruger SR9 9mm pistols

Weapon Purchased Legally? Yes.

Summary: Thornton was employed at the beer distributorship and was captured on video stealing beer. His employers confronted him with the theft, and he went to retrieve two pistols he'd hidden in the business's kitchen. Thornton then walked through the warehouse shooting at people.

Event Ended By: Self-inflicted at the scene.

41. Date: January 8, 2011

Location: U.S. Rep. Gabrielle Giffords Congress on Your Corner, Tucson, AZ

Suspect: Jared Lee Loughner, 22

Killed/Injured: 6 killed, 13 injured

Weapon Used in Incident: GLOCK 19 9mm pistol

Weapon Purchased Legally? Yes.

Summary: U.S. Representative Gabrielle Giffords was conducting a meet-and-greet at a local grocery store when a mentally disturbed subject carrying a handgun attempted to kill her. Loughner fired off approximately thirty rounds in fifteen seconds, shooting Giffords in the head, killing a federal judge, a nine-year-old little girl, and several others. A CNN report, March 28 2013, reveals that Loughner's parents were so worried about his behavior in the weeks leading up to the attack that they disabled his vehicle at night and took his shotgun away.

Event Ended By: According to a NY Daily News article, January 10 2011, multiple bystanders tackled Loughner to the ground and ended the rampage. The article lists their names as **ROGER SALZGEBER, BILL BADGER, DANIEL HERNANDEZ, JOE ZAMUDIO,** and a 61-year-old woman named **PATRICIA MAISCH.**

Loughner was sentenced to life in prison.

Gabby Giffords survived the assassination attempt on her life, despite massive brain injuries. She retired from Congress and according to a Today.com article, January 9, 2014, she marked the three-year anniversary of the shooting like a true survivor. She went skydiving.

42. Date: July 7, 2011

Location: Grand Rapids, MI

Suspect: Rodrick Shonte Dantzler, 34

Killed/Injured: 7 killed, 2 injured

Weapon Used in Incident: GLOCK 9mm pistol

Weapon Purchased Legally? No. Gun was reported stolen from a house two years prior. It remains unknown how Dantzler acquired it.

Summary: NYCCC classifies this as a mass shooting, but I disagree. It occurred in multiple locations and Dantzler knew all of his victims, except for two people he encountered in a road rage incident during his event. According to an NBC news article dated July 8, 2011, Dantzler was targeting his ex-girlfriends. He killed two of them and their family members, including his own 12-year-old little girl. After a police chase, he broke into a house and took three people hostage. Police contained the location and initiated communication.

Event Ended By: Self-inflicted during hostage negotiation.

43. Date: September 6, 2011

Location: Carson City IHOP, Carson City, NV

Suspect: Eduardo Sencion, 32

Killed/Injured: 4 killed, 7 injured

Weapon Used in Incident: Norinco AK-47 type assault rifle

Weapon Purchased Legally? Unknown. According to article by NBC News Investigations dated Sep 7 2011, it is unknown how Sencio acquired the weapon. Norinco sales were banned since 1994. The weapon was modified to full auto.

Summary: According to a Huffington Post article, November 3, 2011, Sencion was a paranoid schizophrenic who was afraid demons were coming after him. He'd been voluntarily and involuntarily committed at various times, and prior to the shooting, he approached family members and priests to ask them for help. On the day of the incident, Sencion walked into a Carson City IHOP and began shooting at diners. He killed multiple people, including three uniformed members of the National Guard. In the parking lot, he shot a woman trying to flee, and then returned to his car.

Event Ended By: Sencion self-inflicted at the scene.

44. Date: July 20, 2012

Location: Century Movie Theater, Aurora, CO

Suspect: James Holmes, 24

Killed/Injured: 12 killed, 58 injured

Weapon Used in Incident: A Smith & Wesson M&P15 assault rifle, a Remington Model 870 12-gauge shotgun, and two GLOCK .40 handguns

Weapon Purchased Legally? Yes.

Summary: According to a NY Daily News article, July 18, 2013, James Holmes was a scholar. He graduated college and received a federal grant for full tuition to the University of Colorado's neuroscience program. It didn't last long. He failed a major exam and withdrew from the program after less than a year, approximately one month prior to the shooting. Holmes was in treatment with a psychiatrist and had no criminal record, but he began amassing explosives and firearms.

On the night of the event, he rigged detonators to explosives set in his apartment that were designed to go off if someone approached. He blared music inside the apartment, hoping to lure someone in and set off the bombs, in order to divert police to the fire while he was on his way to the Century movie theater.

According to an LA Times article, July 20 2012, Holmes came into theater Number 9 through the emergency exit, which was located at the front, near the screen. He was dressed in a riot helmet and gas mask, and he tossed a canister of tear gas into the seats and started firing.

4. Date: April 23, 1987

Location: Palm Bay shopping center, Palm Bay, FL

Suspect: William Cruse, Jr., 59

Killed/Injured: 6 killed, 10 injured

Weapon Used in Incident: Strum, Ruger Mini-14 assault rifle, a shotgun of unknown make and model, and a pistol of unknown make and model.

Weapon Purchased Legally? Yes.

Summary: Cruse was a retiree living with his sick wife. According to an article published in the Los Angeles Times, April 25 1987, his wife told him someone had just run through their yard. The same article mentions that Cruse's neighbors had previously filed a petition against him for tearing down laundry lines and chasing kids when they came too close to his house. One fourteen-year-old boy reported Cruse had once fired warning shots over children's heads to scare them away.

After hearing people were in his yard again, he exited the house with several weapons and shot a teenage boy who was playing basketball nearby. He then drove to the Palm Bay shopping center and killed six people, including two police officers, neither of whom had more than one year on the job.

Event Ended By: Police surrounded the area, and the ensuing standoff lasted over seven hours. Cruse was eventually captured.

Event Ended By: Responding officers arrested Holmes behind the theater. He surrendered peacefully. He remains in prison, as of this writing, awaiting trial.

45. Date: August 5, 2012

Location: Sikh Temple of Wisconsin, Oak Creek, WI

Suspect: Wade Michael Page, 40

Killed/Injured: 6 killed, 3 injured

Weapon Used in Incident: Springfield Armory XD(M) 9mm handgun

Weapon Purchased Legally? Yes.

Summary: According to a Washington Post article dated August 6, 2012, Page was a US Army veteran who was "not eligible for reenlistment" and a white supremacist. He killed six people at the Sikh temple near Milwaukee on the day of the incident and fired multiple times at 51-year-old police lieutenant **BRIAN MURPHY** who arrived at the scene and was attempting to assist another victim.

Event Ended By: According to a Huffington Post article dated August 6, 2012, Lt. **MURPHY** was shot between eight or nine times at close range, including once in the neck. Other Oak Creek police officers soon arrived and located the shooter and ended the threat. When those officers realized **MURPHY** was grievously injured, he waved them off and instructed them to go help the other victims. Page self-inflicted at the scene.

46. Date: September 27, 2012

Location: Accent Signage Systems, Minneapolis, MN

Suspect: Andrew John Engeldinger, 36

Killed/Injured: 6 killed, 2 injured

Weapon Used in Incident: GLOCK 19 9mm pistol

Weapon Purchased Legally? Yes.

Summary: Upon being told he was being fired from his job at Accent Signage, Engeldinger pulled out a gun and shot both his managers. He then shot multiple other people inside the building.

Event Ended By: Self-inflicted at the scene.

47. Date: December 14, 2012

Location: Sandy Hook Elementary School, Newtown, CT

Suspect: Adam Lanza, 20

Killed/Injured: 27 killed, 2 injured

Weapon Used in Incident: An unknown make and model .22-caliber rifle, a Bushmaster XM15 .223-caliber assault rifle, and a GLOCK 10mm handgun

Weapon Purchased Legally? No. Purchased for him by his mother.

Summary: Even after all that, I am still having trouble writing about Sandy Hook. It's difficult reading the accounts of the event and the victims. Especially in terms of trying to be impartial. Occasionally, I'll stumble across articles written by conspiracy-theorists claiming to be able to prove the event was a hoax and, even though I know I shouldn't, I wind up reading the damn things. That's a mistake, because seeing such extreme stupidity and gullibility takes a supreme act of willpower for me not to spend the next five chapters ranting about the state of education in this country. Maybe some other time.

Still, I would be remiss not to point out a few important details about Sandy Hook that will benefit our understanding of mass shootings. Like any tough crime scene or heart-breaking investigation, it is our duty to the victims to stand up in the face of that horror and discern what is true.

According to a Time magazine article dated November 25, 2013, and the Connecticut State's Attorney's Office report detailing the findings of their investigation into the events at Sandy Hook, here is what is true:

Prior to the event, Adam Lanza was doing what we are now. He was reviewing articles and books about previous mass murders and how they occurred, with a special focus on Columbine. He had a spreadsheet to keep track of the shootings, no doubt tallying the body count and what locations yielded the highest numbers and what weapons were used. *(*That is speculation on my part. All that the official report says is that there was information about each of the shootings, but I feel it is an educated guess that the information they mean is what I've listed.)*

For all that pundits like to say that Adam Lanza was addicted to violent video games, such as first-person shooters, there was a GPS in his bedroom that showed he took multiple trips to a local theater to play "Dance Dance Revolution." In fact, they found screen shots of that video game and video of Lanza playing the game when they searched his digital media. In addition to that, he had comedy videos, pictures of hamsters, and things he'd built with Legos.

That is not to say that Lanza wasn't interested in violent video games. They found an independently-created computer game called "School Shooting" on his computer, as well as videos of suicides by gunshots and dramatizations of children being shot.

They also found research Lanza was conducting into pedophilia and the rights of pedophiles.

Finally, they found a check written by Lanza's mother on Christmas 2012 for him to buy a CZ 83 firearm.

It's convenient to slap a label on someone like Adam Lanza to explain his actions. He's a violent video game freak. That must be it. He has Asperger syndrome and was off his meds. That explains it.

As a populace seeking some shred of explanation to help us untangle the sheer horror of an event like Sandy Hook, we desperately latch on to anything they throw at us. The talking heads spew out opinions and theories like chewed tobacco and everybody looks at one another knowingly, confident they've untangled the mystery. Reality is far trickier. If I had to guess, I would say Adam Lanza's actions on that day were the result of a long and complicated series of factors. For whatever reason, the centrifuge reached critical mass that day. On December 14, 2012, Lanza killed his mother while she slept in her bed. We can never know if she was the first target of his rage or he killed her to keep her from being upset over his planned attack, as other shooters had done.

What we do know is that at approximately 0930 hours, he parked his vehicle in a "No Parking" zone outside of Sandy Hook and gathered his weapons. The school's front doors were locked, but Lanza shot out the plate glass windows beside the lobby doors and walked through. That is when the massacre began.

Now, you remember when I spoke about Columbine before? How the police waited for forty-nine minutes to make entry into the school? As we all know, police at the time were trained to secure the scene and wait for SWAT, but since then our tactics had changed. They'd been modified. We now had the "tactical diamond" and other techniques designed to send a small element of police officers into an active shooter situation and deal with it. Did it work? Let's see.

911 dispatched the Newtown Police Department to the scene at 0936 hours.

The first officer arrived in the area behind the school at 0939 hours. Two more arrived within the next thirteen seconds, and gunshots can be heard in the background of their radio transmissions.

The last gunshot is heard inside the school at 0940 hours.

Police did not enter the school until 0944.

Event Ended By: Self-inflicted at the scene.

Now, anybody can Monday morning quarterback any job in the world. It's easy from the safety of our homes or offices and we're not on scene and are not experiencing what is happening directly. I do not say these things to belittle or chastise the cops at Sandy Hook, or the cops at Columbine. I say them because they are true, and that is the currency we trade in as police investigators.

The State's Attorney called the police's actions appropriate because, as the report is careful to point out, they believed there was more than one shooter. They had detained someone outside who was seen running down the street, and located the suspect's car, and that's all well and good but the fact remains that cops were standing outside of the scene while a madman with a gun was inside an elementary school killing women and children.

Listen, I don't know any of the cops who were there that day. I can't imagine the horror they encountered inside that school. Cannot fathom it. Neither can most of you. Blame for the incident can be cut up by Monday morning quarterbacks like sections of a pie and handed out to whatever guilty parties they want, but the fact is, Adam Lanza was responsible.

He was the bad guy. End of discussion.

It's just a shame that particular bad guy was never confronted by the good guys who were right outside.

FIVE: A Conversation with Andy Brown, the Hero of Fairchild

As of 2013, the United States was engaged in at least five wars. According to Harvard's Linda Bilmes and UCLA's Michael Intriligator, at that time we were fighting in Iraq, Afghanistan, Pakistan, Yemen and Somalia. Those were just the ones we were admitting to. They were also in addition to the multiple peace keeping missions and areas of responsibility we oversee in every part of the world.

At home, we are positively jam-packed with soldiers. Hundreds of thousands of military personnel and support staff stationed in bases all across the country. Different people of different backgrounds and training and responsibilities, all engaged in the incomprehensibly massive task of keeping the American military operational.

I'm sure you can imagine that by engaging in such *enthusiastic* deployments of personnel, factored in with what could be considered interference with multiple cultures, religions, and governments, we might make a few enemies along the way. Now, we already know that workplaces experience mass violence because unstable employees see them as a target of their vengeance. We know that places with large clusters of people, such as malls or movie theaters, experience violence because it is guaranteed that the shooter will rack up a high body count. We also know that schools are vulnerable to mass shootings, because nobody has the ability to fight back against a lunatic with a gun.

And every single thing I just said is also true for military bases and facilities stationed here in the United States. They have the attention of our enemies. They are the employers of hundreds of thousands of people, some of whom may be experiencing mental imbalance. There are normally large clusters of people at those locations at any given time. And almost none of them has a gun.

None of the soldiers working on military bases or facilities in the United States is allowed to carry a concealed weapon. Sure, there are guards and private armed security forces and fences and locked doors and security cameras. In theory, it should be one of the safest places on the planet, but in the past ten years, they've been the site of four mass shootings. There was Fairchild in 1994, Fort Hood in 2009, the NAVSEA building in 2013, and again at Fort Hood in 2014.

Three of the four incidents did not involve assault weapons. All were committed by single suspects. And here is another interesting fact. Every single one was ended by the arrival of armed police who engaged the suspect.

As I began to research mass shootings in the United States, I was truly struck by the heroics performed by people confronted with a mass shooter. Some were intended victims who happened to be in the wrong place at the wrong time. Some were men and women holding the True Blue Line who answered the call.

On June 20, 1994, Andrew Brown answered the call.

SCHAFFER: Andy, tell me about your life prior to June 20, 1994.

BROWN: *I graduated high school in 1988 and joined the Air Force as a law enforcement specialist in February 1989. I was stationed in Mt Home, Idaho for about a year. Then at Iraklion Air Station, Crete, Greece, for three years. In 1993 I went to Fairchild AFB, Spokane, Washington. So on June 20, 1994, I had been a patrolman for about five years.*

SCHAFFER: What drove you to join the military, or to be a military policeman?

BROWN: *After high school I had no desire or money for college. I had no interest in a corporate or office type job. I knew I wanted a job in public service such as a firefighter or law enforcement and at age 18, I saw the military as the best option to get into one of those fields. I was also hoping to "see the world."*

SCHAFFER: Have you always been interested in law enforcement?

BROWN: *From reading a little bit of Way of the Warrior, it seems you and I have a similar story. As a kid, my friends and I rode around on our bicycles catching bad guys and saving lives playing motorcycle cop like the California Highway Patrol on the T.V. show "CHiPs." I also emulated the lifesaving firefighters on the T.V. show "Emergency." Firefighters and policemen were my heroes but the cops carried guns and I had a fascination with firearms. I regularly carried a die cast toy replica of a 1911 Colt .45 in the pocket of my jeans. At age seven my dad bought me a second-hand Daisy lever action BB gun. I never considered shooting anything other than pop cans and pinecones and was saddened when I saw the man next door shoot crows and robins with his pellet gun.*

I went through several jobs in my high school years earning just enough to put gas in my motorcycle and camp out at the lake with my buddies. I bused tables and washed dishes at a Denny's, I flipped burgers at the A&W and mounted tires and pumped gas at the 76 gas station near Highway 16. I was working alone one afternoon when an unshaven man whose face and mechanics overalls were blackened with engine grease, walked up from the highway.
His truck had broken down and he needed a fuse but had left home without his wallet. I bought him a box of fuses and he thanked me and walked back down the road. The following day after school I showed up for work and my co-worker told me the State Patrol had been looking for me. He smiled and pointed to a business card and a dollar bill pinned to a bulletin board. The stranded motorist I had helped was Trooper Otto with the Washington State Patrol and he had come back to repay me for the fuses.
As an inexperienced driver I had several opportunities to meet quite a few law enforcement officers and had always admired and respected them as they issued me tickets for various traffic offenses. Up until that day I viewed police officers as flawless super heroes. Seeing Trooper Otto on his day off made me realize that although they have an extraordinary job, law enforcement officers are ordinary people. I started to think that maybe I could become a police officer.
SCHAFFER: That's funny. My first thought that I might become a police officer happened while I was working at a gas station, too. Is anyone in your family a soldier or a cop?

BROWN: *My grandfather was in the Navy, as was my dad before he became a firefighter for the City of Bremerton. My uncles on my mom's side were both military. My older brother went into the Army and my older sister joined the Air Force. My stepfather Stan Barker had been a Marine and worked Law Enforcement in Sea-Tac before I met him.*

SCHAFFER: Where did you grow up?

BROWN: *I was born in 1970 and grew up in the waterfront town of Port Orchard, Washington. Our house was next to a wooded piece of State land and starting at age seven, my friends and I spent most of our days in the woods. We played a lot of war. Dressed in our army surplus uniforms, patrolling the trails along the creek and battling imaginary armies with plastic M16 rifles.*

SCHAFFER: Had you ever experienced violence on the job before that day in Fairchild?

BROWN: *I had responded to a few violent domestic disputes and the occasional bar fight or assault. I'd seen people with serious injuries that resulted from motor vehicle accidents but hadn't personally experienced much traumatic violence.*

SCHAFFER: What was the most serious call or situation you had to deal with as an MP prior to Fairchild?

BROWN: *Our job was similar to that of a small town cop. We worked traffic and speed enforcement, DUI's, domestics, assaults, thefts, shoplifting, vandalism, traffic collisions. There were busy shifts and then there were days when nothing happened unless you went looking for it. I worked with some good cops and learned what I could from them. We worked in isolated locations with* *environments that tolerated complacency, and peers who scoffed at officer-safety tactics. At times the hardest part of our job was maintaining a survival mindset. I chose not to emulate the cops who had allowed themselves to become complacent.*

SCHAFFER: What would you say is the best part of your training that prepared you to survive and win at Fairchild?

BROWN: *Our primary mission was Air Base Defense so the majority of our formal training focused on resource protection, primarily the flight line and aircraft. Law Enforcement was considered a secondary mission and in my opinion the training was minimal. There were some dedicated individuals who worked in the Training Section but their funding and resources were limited. I didn't feel adequately trained but I didn't know what was missing or where to find it.*

A couple years into my career I found what I was missing in books like The Tactical Edge: Surviving High-Risk Patrol by Charles Remsberg, and Street Survival: Tactics for Armed Encounters by Ronald J. Adams, Thomas M. McTernan and Charles Remsberg. The authors had interviewed officers who survived lethal encounters and compiled their experience and street wisdom regarding officer safety, tactics and mindset. The books helped me learn to think like a cop.

The books also taught me the technique of mental rehearsal, that I believe helped prepare me for the shooting. In the same way an athlete visualizes the movements toward the goal of their sport, I started visualizing lethal force scenarios. Before I went to sleep I'd lie in bed and mentally rehearse a lethal force encounter. Whether it was a traffic stop, armed robbery, or domestic dispute, I'd see the subject threaten me or someone else. I'd slowly visualize my action to counter and terminate the threat. Every night I imagined a different scenario and when I had down time during my shift I played the "What If" game. What if this happens, how would I react? What if that happens? What would I do? What would be good cover from gunfire if something happened right now? Where is the best exit route if I need to retreat?

After a real world incident, traffic stop or any other encounter with the public, I'd critique my own tactics. "Had I left myself vulnerable at any point? What could I have done better or safer?"

It's something I still work on today.

I continued to be courteous and professional, but learned to approach everyone with the thought that they intended to do me harm.

SCHAFFER: One of the things that stands out to me about the Fairchild incident is that you shot Mellberg from so far away. The maximum distance police officers qualify at with handguns in PA is 25 yards. Hitting a living target with a handgun at 70 yards is absolutely astounding, and yet, you did it twice. Have you always been a good marksman?

BROWN: *As a kid I was a decent shot, plinking with BB guns and the occasional .22 rifle. I didn't have any training or the opportunity to shoot many handguns prior to joining the Air Force.*

SCHAFFER: How well did training at the range prepare you for the encounter with Mellberg?

BROWN: *We qualified every six months with the Beretta M9 and I believe our maximum training range was also 25 yards. It was all paper silhouette targets, not much shoot-don't-shoot training. Our Combat Arms Training and Maintenance instructors did an excellent job of teaching us the basic fundamentals of marksmanship, controlling your breathing, and trigger control. Shortly after becoming familiar with the M9 I regularly qualified as an expert marksman.*

Our issued weapons were stored in the armory and we were only allowed to carry when we were on duty. I wanted more trigger time than the Air Force could give me so I bought a used Taurus 92, an affordable replica of the M9. I wanted to be able to practice on my own time with a weapon that was functionally identical to the one we carried on duty. A few of my buddies and I went out into the woods near the base for target practice which usually consisted of putting holes in plastic bottles and pop cans. I did practice some longer range shots, but being familiar with the weapon and practicing the fundamentals until it was second nature was key to my winning the gunfight. Once I made the decision to fire I didn't have to think about it, it just happened. **SCHAFFER:** What was your day like prior to being dispatched to the shooting?

BROWN: *It was like any other day. I showed up an hour before our shift and went to check my weapon out of the armory. My assigned weapon had been tagged for some sort of maintenance so I was issued a standby gun. It was an identical M9 but one I had never fired before.*

Prior to that day I had always patrolled in a car, Crown Vics and the like but June 20th 1994 was my second shift on Fairchild's newly formed Bicycle Patrol.

It was a swing shift, meaning we worked from 1400 to 2200 hrs. It was a cloudless summer day and I spent the first hour patrolling housing areas on base. As I rode down the sidewalks and through the streets I was greeting folks who were washing cars and mowing lawns and I waved to the kids who were playing in sprinklers. I planned to head off base to patrol two housing areas that sat just outside the perimeter fence on either side of our base hospital.

The hospital and housing areas were on land that the Air Force leased from the county. There was no perimeter fence around the area and we had concurrent jurisdiction with the Spokane County Sheriff Office. On my way out the gate I stopped to visit the gate guard and was resting in the air conditioned gate shack when the call came over our radios.

SCHAFFER: How was the call dispatched?

BROWN: *Our Desk Sergeant had just finished training to be a dispatcher. It was one of his first shifts working alone on the desk and he handled it like a pro. At least three phone lines rang simultaneously along with the hospital Emergency Room duress alarm.* (All of the audio is at Andy's website: Fairchildhospitalshooting.com on the Police Audio page.)

The first phone the Desk Sergeant picked up was dead on the other end. He picked up the Crime Stop line and said, "Crime Stop, are you reporting a crime or emergency?"

The caller replied, "Uh, emergency crime there's a guy in the hospital running around with a shotgun."
The Desk Sergeant immediately put the call out on the radio.
"Fairchild Police to all Posts and Patrols, we have an alarm, at the ER hospital. Informational, we have an individual in the hospital running around with a shotgun."
SCHAFFER: I'll tell you a secret. It's not something I'm proud of, but I've been dispatched to a few major incidents that made it hard for me to breathe when I tried talking on the radio. I don't know if it's fear or adrenaline or what, but when you're on your way to a call of someone shooting at police or civilians, and there are lights and sirens going, and your mind is racing a million miles a second as you race to get there, it has a physical effect on me that leaves me huffing for air and having trouble speaking clearly on the radio.
I can only imagine what the call you got at Fairchild would have done to me, especially if I was on a bicycle. Do you remember what your mindset was as you responded?
BROWN: *I have had reactions similar to the one you describe but on that day the adrenaline dump affected me differently. There were definite physical reactions in my vision, time perception and hearing but if my motor skills and breathing were affected, I didn't notice it. As I rode toward the area I tried to predict and mentally prepare for what I might encounter and then I just went on auto pilot, focused on quickly getting to the scene.*
SCHAFFER: What are your memories of the firefight?
BROWN: *I have been working on a book so I have a detailed account of my response.*

Radio calls that are directed to "all posts and patrols" are usually urgent so before the transmission ended I had already strapped on my helmet and stepped out of the gate shack to get to my bicycle. The severity of the call set in as I rode away from the gate, imagining what I might encounter as I mentally rehearsed my response.

Was it a disgruntled patient? A jealous husband? A hostage situation? I envisioned arriving at the ER and encountering a gunman threatening others. I saw myself taking cover in the parking lot and shooting to end the threat.

I reached the intersection of Offutt and Graham and was suddenly aware that unlike my patrol car, my bicycle wasn't equipped with lights and a siren. I reached for my duty belt and slipped the key ring off the antenna of my radio. I blew a little chrome whistle that I kept with my keys and turned left onto Graham.

The hospital was a third of a mile away down the straight two lane asphalt road. As I pedaled hard toward the scene, the world around me slowed and went silent like when water gets stuck in your ears. I was calm, almost numb. Several vehicles were headed my way. A car slowed and the driver frantically shouted out his window. I stared at him as I coasted by, his mouth moved in slow-motion and his voice was muted. I didn't stop to figure out what he said.

I kept pedaling toward the hospital as more vehicles fled past me. A slow rolling, military dump truck approached. I saw people standing in the dump bed, others clinging to the cab alongside the passenger door. It reminded me of a parade. Someone leaned over the tall sides of the dump bed waved and yelled down at me as I rode by. I couldn't hear their words, but their urgency and the number of cars leaving the area told me there was trouble ahead.

There was another radio transmission, "Fairchild Police to all responding patrols, the individual just ran out of building 9010 across from the hospital firing off rounds out of his shotgun."

I passed a housing area on my right and saw building 9010 emerging in the distance. A crowd of men and women dressed in civilian clothes, Air Force uniforms and hospital whites, streamed away from the building, moving quickly down the side of the street. I coasted past the crowd scanning them and the surrounding area for a threat. I shouted, "Where is he?"

The crowd collectively pointed behind them as they fled, yelling, "There's a man with a gun!" "He's shooting people!" "He's over there!"

I emerged from the crowd and heard the deep boom of gunfire reverberating off the hospital buildings to my right and the military houses behind the perimeter fence to my left. I coasted and searched for the source of the gunfire. In the distance, a man dressed in black with a long-gun at his hip appeared in the middle of the road.

As he walked toward me, he swung the weapon to his right and fired toward the houses, he continued walking and swung the weapon to his left, firing toward the hospital. I was so focused on the gunman, I hadn't heard the radio, "Fairchild Police, Fairchild Security, just received a notification from the hospital, you have individuals down. Repeat. You have individuals down."

I leaned right and rode up the sidewalk ramp in front of building 9010. I leapt from my bike. Momentum carried me a couple steps forward as I drew my Beretta and knelt on the sidewalk. The bike crashed behind me on a patch of freshly mowed grass. My peripheral vision went black but I was aware of people scrambling to hide in ditches and behind cars. I gripped my pistol with both hands and brought it in line with my target as I yelled, "Police, Drop your weapon! Put it down!"

He continued toward me and fired again to his side. I yelled, "Police! Drop it! Put it down now!" He quickened his pace, moving at an angle toward the parking lot to his left. He aimed his weapon in my direction and fired.

He was far away, so much so that as I aimed my pistol his body was nearly obscured by the steel rectangle of my front sight. I slowly pressed the trigger and fired in a controlled succession, the first three rounds had no effect though one of them had hit him in the shoulder. The fourth round hit him between the eyes.

With great relief, I watched him fall flat on his back the weapon lay at his side in his left hand.

SCHAFFER: The way I've read the newspaper accounts of the Fairchild incident, along with the OSI's report and the Spokane County Sheriff's Office report, Dean Mellberg was chasing people out of the hospital with the intention of shooting them.

BROWN: *He started shooting in the hospital annex and continued firing as he left the annex and crossed the parking lot to the main hospital. He moved through the main floor of the crowded hospital and followed people as they fled out an emergency exit. He pursued people as they moved to cover behind cars and bushes before moving out Graham road, the same road I was on as I responded.*

He walked North down Graham firing at people as they moved ahead of him from one place of cover to another. I responded South down Graham and observed him walking down the middle of the road. I was experiencing tunnel vision and was so focused on stopping him I didn't think about cover and didn't see the steel transformer box or telephone pole nearby as I knelt on the sidewalk. I was wearing my vest but that wouldn't have stopped the 7.62 rounds he was firing.

SCHAFFER: What happened immediately after it ended?

BROWN: *After he fell, I stood up and moved forward to a pickup truck that was parked between me and the shooter. On my way there I realized I hadn't radioed that I was on scene, I keyed my lapel mike and transmitted, "Fairchild, Six, shots fired, I took him down, he's down, this is Police Six, he's down!"*

I used the truck for cover as I waited for back up to arrive. I kept my gun trained on the gunman and yelled, "Don't move!"

He was motionless. I shook off the tunnel vision and quickly scanned left, right and behind for additional threats. I was aware of several people in the area and that others had been wounded but I didn't observe any additional threats. I yelled at the people around me, "Get out of the area. If you aren't a medic get out of the area."

My back up, as well as officers and medical crews from several surrounding agencies, began to arrive. I assisted in securing the perimeter and then aided in searching the main hospital for a rumored second gunman.

As I moved through the hospital, evidence of the violence that had occurred was everywhere. I will never forget searching the hospital cafeteria and the way my black tennis shoes slid across the blood slicked tile floor. That image became more traumatic when I learned that the blood on the floor was from Christin McCarron, an eight-year-old girl who had been killed.

SCHAFFER: Jesus, that's horrifying. What can you tell us about Dean Mellberg?

BROWN: *Like many of those who commit mass public murder, Mellberg exhibited anti-social, paranoid and schizoid behavior. He had an exaggerated perception of injustice. He took offense to benign comments and had a habit of blaming others for the negative consequences of his actions. He had no insight into his mental disorder and felt the military mental health system was being used to persecute him and ruin his Air Force career. He filed several baseless complaints with his supervisors in an attempt to right his perceived injustices. When he lost his military career, his limited coping skills and a mind that wasn't wired right allowed him to resort to homicidal revenge.*

SCHAFFER: What can you tell us about some of the things you experienced in the aftermath of the shooting?

BROWN: *Thankfully, given the circumstances, I never experienced any guilt in taking Mellberg's life. I did second guess myself and my response time. With the time distortion, I had no idea how long it took me to get there and I couldn't help thinking I could have saved more lives if I had gotten there sooner. I was not afforded an opportunity to listen to the police radio recording of the response. I made several FOIA requests for the recording and kept getting denied. Finally, fifteen years after the incident I managed to get a* *copy of the recorded radio traffic. I discovered that less than two minutes had passed between the initial radio call and my radio call that the gunman was down. It wasn't until then that I was able to consider the lives I had saved instead of focusing on the ones I hadn't.*

On the day of the shooting, I was called out to the perimeter and met the Sheriff's Department Detectives who were taking over the investigation. I had to surrender my weapon and my superiors took me from the scene while my partners continued their work securing the hospital.

The night of the incident I couldn't sleep. I was amped up on adrenaline and hyper alert, I laid down to rest but every time I closed my eyes the encounter with the gunman vividly replayed in my head.

I had to work an unarmed position in confinement guarding prisoners until the investigation was complete. That took about four months. When it was officially determined that I acted in defense of self or others, I was allowed to go back on patrol.

I wanted to make sure I was dealing with the incident properly and self-referred to see a counselor but I stopped going when my command relieved me of duty and took away my weapon handling privileges. There was nothing wrong with me mentally and the psychologist was baffled as to why my squadron reacted the way they did, but it was apparent that I could either be a patrolman or see a counselor, not both.

SCHAFFER: Let no good deed go unpunished. Tell me about moving to Hawaii and leaving the service.

BROWN: *I accepted a three-year assignment to Hickam Air Force Base, in Hawaii. I thought I might escape the notoriety of the shooting, but word had already spread. I arrived at my new duty station and was introduced as "The guy who shot that dude at Fairchild."*

I worked as a patrolman and then as an investigator. I began to notice symptoms of Post-Traumatic Stress. I had intrusive thoughts; almost everything reminded me of the incident. I wasn't sleeping well and I became depressed, irritable, anxious and reclusive. I was hyper alert, uncomfortable in crowds and intolerant of noise. I began to rely on alcohol to calm the anxiety and escape.

I eventually sought counseling and was again relieved of duty, so I stuffed it and went back to my duties. The symptoms continued to worsen over time.

In 1998, I received orders to Kirtland Air Force Base in Albuquerque New Mexico where I worked as a patrolman and then once again as an investigator. My symptoms progressed and the job I loved had become another source of anxiety and discomfort. It reached a point that seeing a counselor was worth the price of losing my gun.

After a few months of counseling I realized that talking it out wasn't going to work and I got out of the military hoping to find relief. I returned to Spokane, met my wife, and started a family but I was still struggling.

I went through several industrial laborer jobs and had trouble adapting to civilian life. I watched a lot of news programs and listened to news talk radio that focused on negative topics and issues. Over time the negativity consumed me and I took on a negative view of the world and the people around me. I did my best to hide it but I was anxious and constantly on guard. I was cynical and expected the worst from everyone I interacted with. I was slipping into a dark isolated hole.

I hated the way I felt and read a lot of books and searched the internet looking for anything to resolve my symptoms. I tried medication, meditation, acupuncture, diet and exercise. I saw doctors and counselors and went through programs. Some of those things helped but the relief was temporary. I began to accept that I would never be normal but for the sake of my kids and with the encouragement of my wife I continued to seek peace.

SCHAFFER: And how about now, Andy? Have you made peace with what happened that day?

BROWN: *Yes, I have. Things started to improve in 2009. I started writing a book about the shooting and researching the history behind it. That forced me to repeatedly confront the incident which helped minimize its effect on me. At about that same time I was reading books about mental trauma and also about Mindfulness and Buddhist philosophy I tried to incorporate some of those practices into my life. I worked toward not dwelling on the past or worrying about the future. I made an effort to appreciate the present, simple moments in my life.*

I practiced focusing on and controlling my breath, also known as combat breathing which is very calming. I made a conscious effort to be more empathetic and forgiving of other people. I stopped obsessively following the news and other negative media and I stopped self-medicating with alcohol.

I also enrolled in some relatively new programs at the Spokane, Washington Veterans Administration Medical Center - Prolonged Exposure Therapy and Cognitive Processing Therapy. Among other things my counselor helped me dissect the incident and explore what specifically was bothering me. I learned that my thoughts about the shooting and my thoughts about the world around me were causing my anxiety and other symptoms. I learned how to challenge those thoughts which over time dramatically changed the way I felt and my symptoms began to diminish. It sounds like a simple process but it was a lot of work and it didn't happen overnight. It's an ongoing effort but it works.

I am not disillusioned, I know there is evil in the world and I am still vigilant, but I have learned to practice a more balanced awareness. I no longer see only the negative. I can once again see and appreciate the beauty in the world while I am looking for the danger.

SCHAFFER: What kind of hearings or inquiries did you have to participate in as a result of Fairchild?

BROWN: *My only participation in the investigation was an interview with the Sheriff's detectives three days after the shooting. They were thorough and professional and did a good job of articulating the facts that showed it was a good shoot.*

SCHAFFER: On your website, and in your forthcoming book, you discuss making contact with the families of the victims and survivors of the Fairchild shooting. What drove you to contact them?

BROWN: *I knew that if I was struggling with the trauma that they certainly must have been also. Initially I reached out to them to see how they were and learn how they were coping. I wanted to bring other survivors together in hope that it would help in the healing effort.*

I have been in touch with many of the people who were in the hospital or responded to it as a medic or law enforcement officer. Few if any escaped without some form of mental trauma.

SCHAFFER: You've got direct experience with a rampage shooter on a different level than most of us will ever come close to. Tell me something, what does modern law enforcement need to know about rampage shooters in order to prepare ourselves for future events?

BROWN: *That information is out there if you search for it. Ron Borsch has a lot of helpful information on the internet and in a newsletter. If you look up Lt. Dan Marcou, he has some good insight as well. Policeone.com is a good resource for all things law enforcement.*

I like to read about police lethal force incidents, not to second guess the officer's actions, because I wasn't there and don't know what they knew or didn't know at the time. Instead, I look at the scenario and think about what I would do in that situation, so that I might be better prepared if I encounter something similar in the future.

The Modern Law Enforcement response to rampage shooters is simple, the good guys with the guns need to run to the sound of violence and terminate the threat.

Also remember, no place is immune. It could happen to you and you need to ask yourself beforehand if you are willing to go at it alone and search out an armed attacker. I know there is a lot of focus on going home at the end of your shift. But if you can't commit yourself now to respond as if it was your family member in danger. If you even think you would hesitate to act you need to find another career field. You owe that to yourself, your partners and the people who will be depending on you. Don't wait for back up and when back up does arrive, split up so you can cover more ground.

Be aware that plain clothes LEO's and CCW's might be in the area.

SCHAFFER: In the past five years we've had two rampage killers commit mass murders at Fort Hood, and one at the Washington Navy Yard. What are we doing wrong and what can we do to fix the situation?

BROWN: *These incidents are not new, they have been happening for centuries but we as a society have been slow to learn from history.*

It took me less than two minutes to get the hospital and end the killing. In law enforcement a two minute response time is exceptional but still twenty-six people were shot. In my opinion we need to harden the preferred targets of mass public murder by eliminating the "gun free zones." The law abiding citizens, soldiers or airmen who choose to defend themselves should not be denied the necessary tools to do so.

Also, our mental health care system is broken. The percentage of people with mental illnesses that will become violent is relatively small. However, many of the people who commit this type of crime have paranoid schizophrenic conditions and are so mentally ill that they have no insight into their illness. If treatment is available it isn't mandated unless the person is deemed capable of violence and even then the treatment is only temporarily enforced. Usually the person doesn't realize they are sick so they refuse treatment. They become someone else's problem and many of them end up homeless or in jail or prison. We ignore the problem until the next incident of mass public murder but something needs to change. Our right to live in a safe society should outweigh the violently mentally ill's right to remain sick.

SCHAFFER: I can imagine it gets cumbersome having to always discuss the Fairchild incident. You have much more to contribute than just talking about that one day. What else can you tell me about yourself? Who is Andy Brown, 2014?

BROWN: *It has never bothered me to talk about the shooting, I think it is therapeutic. I have done a lot of research and want to share everything I have learned about the Fairchild shooting in an effort to prevent future incidents and help prepare first responders when they do occur. That is why I decided to write the book. But you are right, there is more to me than being the guy that shot that dude at Fairchild. I am a husband and father. I enjoy firearms and time with my family. I have a good job with the Border Patrol in Spokane and am happy to once again be serving the public. I have devoted a lot of time working on the book and am looking forward to finishing it so I can spend more time with my family and pursue other interests.*

SCHAFFER: Every article, interview, news piece, and reference to you from now until the end of time will call you an American hero. I'm sure you've heard it so much by now that you just wait for people to get it over with. But the reality of it all, Andy, the stone cold truth of the matter, is that if you hadn't done what you did a whole lot more people would have died that day. A whole lot more families would have had to bury their loved ones, but for you. I just want you to know that I, and my readers, and every person who ever hears your story, will be proud and grateful that you were the one who took that call. You deserved your Airman's medal, and much more. On behalf of every man and woman who is holding the blue line, and from the bottom of my heart, thank you.

SIX: Myths and Realities of Confronting Mass Shooters

In 2009, noted criminologist and Florida State University Professor Gary Kleck published a paper called "Mass Shootings in School: The Worst Possible Case for Gun Control." Kleck is neither an NRA hack, nor a gun control apologist. He speaks hard truths about gun control that I'm sure bring little joy to his fellow academics. It was Kleck's paper, which I'd initially read looking for facts backing up my belief that increased gun control would prevent mass school shootings, that caused me to reevaluate my position.

Kleck makes several points in his work that are worth making note of here.

First, he says that the killers who commit mass shootings plan them long in advance. We have seen evidence of that in multiple mass shootings where the killer methodically acquired weapons and studied the actions of previous shooters. Kleck states that gun control methods that delay shooters from acquiring weapons will have little to no effect of the perpetrators of mass school shootings because they will simply wait. They will bide their time and refine their plan.

Second, he says that guns used by rampage killers in these events either already belong to them or are stolen. He even goes on to say that locking mechanisms will prove little use to stop these incidents because rampage killers are highly-motivated and once they have the weapon will find a way to remove it. He does point out that locking your gun can prevent accidental disasters, such as those caused by children firing a gun, but they will not stop mass shooters from stealing the weapon and making it operational.

Third, he says that mass school shooters use multiple guns and carry multiple magazines full of ammo. Restrictions on high-capacity magazines designed to load a single weapon with the maximum amount of ammunition possible will have little effect on deterring rampage killers. They'll simply carry more guns, or multiple magazines.

Fourth, he says that in each of the mass shootings he studied, the killers had enough time to shoot their weapons and kill their victims, regardless of whether they were "Assault Weapons" or not. The amount of time it takes to empty a semi-automatic pistol vs. a so-called assault weapon, and the damage inflicted by either gun, is of marginal difference. He says that a ban on assault weapons will not reduce mass shootings and it will not reduce the body count.

Finally, and I believe this is the most important point Professor Kleck makes, he says that no law can stop a rampage killer. They are too motivated. They are too willing to die in order to carry out their plan.

Mother Jones is a non-profit news organization that focuses on investigative journalism, as well as political and social justice issues. They also maintain a large database on mass shootings and the specific aspects of each incident.

According to Mother Jones, 49 of the weapons used in mass shootings between 1982 and 2012 were obtained legally. 12 were not. 71 were committed with handguns. That is one less than all the mass shootings committed with rifles, revolvers, and shotguns combined.

Now, that is not to say that gun control laws are ineffective. In fact, according to an article by researcher Richard Florida that appeared in The Atlantic on January 13, 2011, his analysis of states with strict gun control laws have significantly lower rates of death by firearms. Other factors that seem to influence the rate of death include the wealth of the community and the amount of college graduates.

That all certainly makes sense. Show me a neighborhood where everybody has money and went to college and I'm going to show you neighborhood that is not afflicted by a multitude of ailments that other, less fortunate communities are. Furthermore, for gun control laws to pass in any state, its voters clearly are willing to support the politicians passing the legislation. I'm going to go out on a limb here and guess that those voters weren't too keen on guns to begin with, so there probably aren't as many guns as you'd find in places like Pennsylvania or Texas.

Of course, strict gun laws are not the answer in every circumstance.

Washington D.C. has stricter gun control laws than most other states in the country. You cannot carry a gun in Washington, either in the open or concealed. Assault weapons are banned. They have a 10 day waiting period to buy firearms. Guns have to be registered and re-registered on a regular basis, and anyone wanting to own a gun has to comply with a background check and take an online safety course. Also, there is a multitude of gun free zones.

And yet, since 1994, Washington D.C. has been the scene of multiple high-profile shootings, including those we previously discussed. As recently as 2013, a rampage killer named Aaron Alexis entered the NAVSEA building in D.C. with a shotgun and a 9mm Beretta, killed twelve innocent people, and injured eight more.

According to a Washington Post article dated February 21, 2014, it took 170 police officers who fought a total of eight different gun battles with Alexis to stop him. Ending the fight finally fell to Officer **DORIAN DeSANTIS**, who was shot in the chest before returning fire and removing Alexis from the census count.

Ask yourself this. If posted signs are so good at restricting illegal behavior, why do we still have speeding? Or trespassing? Or loitering? Or illegal parking? Sure, for the most part, they work. They act as advisories to all the honest people out there of what they should and should not do. But are they totally effective? Of course not.

So what are we really preventing with gun-free zones in various areas? What are we accomplishing aside from keeping the honest people unarmed and announcing to all the potential mass shooters and rampaging psychopaths where they can go in order to rack up a high number of fatalities?

Remember, these are people who intend to die anyway. They aren't worried about the consequences of being caught.

Now, if all of that that is true, we must ask ourselves the only question that matters. If gun control and restrictions on types of weapons and background checks and gun-free zones will not work on rampage shooters, what in the hell will?

You will.

How do I know this? Simple. It's worked a few times before.

One of the things the NRA and gun control advocates love to argue about are incidents where armed citizens were able to stop mass shootings before they occurred. Both sides roll out various experts and counter each other in an ongoing bickerfest that does little except placate their mentally-dull supplicants. But there is one interesting aspect about the argument and it comes from the gun control side.

While the NRA uses these incidents to pump up auditoriums full of Pennsyltucky hillbillies eager to supply their militia with Gatling guns and rocket launchers, the gun control people want it known that a majority of the time, when a so-called armed citizen intervened in a mass shooting and won, that individual was actually a cop or military personnel. A well-trained, armed, mentally-prepared member of the modern warrior class who rose to the occasion.

Are you listening to me, NRA Lifetime Members who get the magazine every month and display the bumper stickers and wear the baseball hats proclaiming your membership? The ones who push one button in the voting booth? The ones who would rather catch cancer than agree with somebody who supports gun control? Pay attention. I'm using small words so even the knuckleheads in my own family can understand me. The gun control advocates want us to be armed because even they believe we are the only ones who can stop these events.

On January 16, 2002, a 42-year-old Nigerian former student rampaged at the Appalachian School of Law in Grundy, VA, with a .380 pistol. He killed the dean, a teacher, a student, and wounded three others before being subdued. The gun-nuts love to say it was "armed students" who intervened. A Mother Jones article dated December 12, 2002, states that they are conveniently forgetting the armed students were actually cops.

A NY Times article dated January 17, 2002, describes how Officer **MIKAEL GROSS** grabbed his bulletproof vest and gun from his car before he tackled the shooter. He was assisted by former police officers **TRACY BRIDGES** and **TED BENSEN.**

On December 9, 2007, failed seminary student Matthew Murray went on a rampage in Colorado. At approximately 0030 hours, he attacked the Youth With A Mission training center in Arvada and killed two people. He wounded two others before he escaped. At approximately 1300 hours, he attacked the New Life Church, located approximately sixty-five miles away in Colorado Springs. He shot and killed two teenage girls in the parking lot and wounded their father. He shot two more people before trying to make entry into the sanctuary, when he met fate in the form of **JEANNE ASSAM.**

ASSAM was a former police officer who volunteered to guard the church that day after hearing about the youth center shootings. According to an ABC news report on December 12, 2007, Murray went into the church heavily armed and had likely posted in an online forum earlier that day that he was coming to kill "everyone." At the time he went into that sanctuary full of people, he was carrying a Bushmaster XM15 assault rifle, a .40 Beretta and a 9mm Springfield.

ASSAM had a Beretta 9mm and ten rounds, but she used them effectively and ended the fight. According to an LA Times article dated December 11, 2007, **ASSAM** shot Murray multiple times, saving an unknown amount of lives.

On February 12, 2007, an 18-year-old Bosnian immigrant named Sulejman Talović attacked the Trolley Square mall in Salt Lake City, Utah, with a shotgun and a .38 revolver. He killed five people and injured four more before off duty police officer **KENNETH HAMMOND** intervened. According to a Fox News story dated February 14, 2007, **HAMMOND** was enjoying an early Valentine's Day dinner with his wife when he left her and engaged the shooter.

(At Valentine's Day dinner with his wife, I said. Armed. This is a man *committed* to protecting and serving.)

A Salt Lake Tribune article dated March 25, 2012, gives further details of how **HAMMOND** and Salt Lake City Sgt. **ANDY OBLAD** exchanged shots with Talović and backed him into a Pottery Barn. SWAT officers then came up from the rear and ended the event.

On May 27, 2010, a 79-year-old named Abraham Dickan walked into an AT&T store in New York Mills, NY, with a list of six names. According to a WKTV News article that same day, it was a list of employees he intended to kill. He'd been in the store several times before and was extremely angry at the people on his list, and that was the day he was going to take revenge. In fact, as soon as he walked in, he shot one employee with a .357 Magnum. Dickan was just getting started when off-duty officer **DONALD MOORE**, who was shopping in the same store, drew his weapon and fired, killing the gunman.

On December 16, 2012, 19-year-old Jesus Manuel Garcia opened fire at the Santikos Mayan Palace 14 Theater in San Antonio, TX. According to a CBS article dated December 17, 2012, Garcia began shooting inside a nearby restaurant and then continued into the movie theater parking lot. He shot a pedestrian and a marked police car and was headed into the movie theater when an off-duty police officer shot him and put him down.

A KENS5 News article dated December 19, 2012, describes how Sgt. **LISA CUELLO CASTELLANO** was awarded the Medal of Valor for her actions. It also says that another off-duty officer, **ARMONDO OLGUIN**, came out of a theater at the sound of gunshots and helped make the arrest.

We've already discussed the Pearl High School shooting where Assistant Principal **JOEL MYRICK** intervened and grabbed his gun from his truck, but not the unidentified US Marine who stopped a mass shooter at a Winnemucca bar in May, 2008.

According to an Elko Daily Free Press article dated May 24, 2008, a 30-year-old named Ernesto Villagomez pulled out a handgun and killed two brothers inside the bar. He injured two other people before someone else inside the bar, a 49-year-old soldier, drew his gun and put the shooter down.

If you read the pro-gun accounts of these stories, they'll gloss over the fact that the people involved with these incidents were cops or soldiers, and if you read the pro-gun control accounts, they basically say, "So what? That's what cops are supposed to do."

Now, if you want to see some real shenanigans, take a look at the way incidents where untrained civilians with a gun have tried to intervene with a rampage shooter are twisted and turned by both sides. They will argue about anything. They'll argue whether the CCW intervened too late, or that the shooter did not "intend" to shoot anyone else and it wouldn't have mattered. They'll argue about whether the event was actually a mass shooting and not just some domestic incident gone haywire. They'll pull out every "expert" or former federal agent willing to give them a good quote and slap that quote as far as the eye can see, saying, "See! See! I'm right!"

But here's the facts.

In all the mass shootings we've ever had, only one appears to have been ended by an untrained civilian using force. Not military, not law enforcement, not former either of those things, just a regular guy who took action. And here's the kicker. He didn't kill the bad guy with a gun. He killed him with his car.

Well, let me back up. He did shoot the bad guy. Then he used the car to finish the job.

On August 20, 1982, Carl Brown, a 51 year old teacher with a history of mental problems bicycled to Bob Moore's Welding Shop in Miami and killed eight people with a 12-gauge shotgun. **MARK KRAM,** who was working at his own shop not far away, heard of the shootings and jumped in his car with two guns.

According to a NY Times article dated August 24, 1982, **KRAM** caught up to the fleeing gunman, who was pedaling away from the scene on his bike, and shot him in the back. Then, **KRAM** hit Brown with the car and knocked him into a light pole. Then-Dade State's Attorney Janet Reno told the press that no charges were going to be filed against **KRAM.**

Another incident of civilian intervention occurred on April 24, 1998, when Andrew Wurst, a 14-year-old took his father's .25 pistol to a middle school dance in Edinboro, PA. The dance was being held at Nick's Place, a hall owned by **JAMES STRAND.** According to a Philly.com article posted April 26, 1998, Wurst murdered one of the teachers chaperoning the dance and fired on another teacher and two students. **STRAND** grabbed a shotgun and went after Wurst, who had fled the building. **STRAND** caught Wurst and held him until responding officers could arrive.

It hasn't always gone so well.

On February 4, 2005, a man named David Hernandez Arroyo, Sr. confronted his ex-wife and adult son in front of the Smith County Courthouse in Tyler, TX. He shot the woman and killed her with an AK-47-type rifle and shot his son. Uniformed officers exchanged gunfire with the suspect, who was wearing body armor.

According to a KWTX News article dated February 25, 2005, a bystander named **MARK ALAN WILSON** attempted to intervene but was killed by Arroyo. Smith County's Sheriff credited **WILSON** with saving one of the intended victims, Arroyo, Jr., from being murdered. A KLTV News article states that **WILSON** fired several shots at Arroyo using his concealed firearm.

Police ultimately pursued Arroyo, and after exchanging fire, Tyler Police Sgt. **RUSTY JACKS** killed the suspect.

On November 20, 2005, a 20-year-old named Dominick Sergio Maldonado walked down the corridors of the Tacoma Mall, shooting people with a Norinco Mak-90 assault rifle and a pistol. He injured multiple people, and in the midst of his spree, he was confronted by the assistant manager of a gift shop. **BRENDAN "DAN" McKOWN** drew his 9mm pistol and attempted to subdue the shooter. Maldonado shot first and hit **McKOWN** multiple times. According to a Seattle Times article published May 6, 2006, **McKOWN** is paralyzed and uses a wheelchair. He talks about feeling humiliated and failing to protect people.

Respectfully, I disagree with him.

Things don't always work out, and our tactics sometimes fail. It doesn't lessen the noble intent of a citizen who chooses to engage the enemy rather than running and hiding. Long after the medals and commendations are handed out to police officers for their actions, **DAN McKOWN** will still be in a wheelchair. **MARK WILSON** will still be dead. They deserve better than to be turned into fodder for journalists and lobbyists who will feed us all into the threshing machine of publicity for their cause.

As I finished this chapter last night I heard the news that there had been yet another mass shooting in Santa Barbara, CA. Another committed with legally purchased handguns, another taking place in the vicinity of a school. The shooter was, in the words of one of my favorite eighties movies, "just another asshole, mad at the world."

I've since watched the usual parade of comments, pleas, and postings roll out via social media. People pray for peace and for the victims, others cajole and harass the NRA. The NRA, for its part, maintains a policy of staying mum for a few days after a mass shooting. Before long, they'll be holding a press conference and declaring we'd all be a lot safer if we could just have more guns. The media scours the dregs of the internet to find the vilest comments agreeing with the shooter, if only to remind people that no matter how low we go, there is always room to sink lower. It's an orgy of media coverage, talking heads, political jockeying and internet commentary.

And somewhere, in the background of all of that, are innocent lives we handed over without a fight. Every time another one of these psychopaths take the life of one of our children, our wives, our husbands, our teachers, our police officers, our future, they are stealing it and we keep handing them over.

This much is certain.

We will never solve the gun rights/gun control issue. That's not our job. We will never solve the mental health issue that goes hand in hand with so many of these rampage shooters. That is also not our job.

We will never solve the phenomenon of terrorism, rampage shooters, serial killers, or any of the horrors that exist in our society. That is an impossibly big task and not our job.

Our job is to be ready when one of them shows up. When these serpents rear their heads, we cut them off, or we press them to the ground under the heel of our boot and defang them so they can't hurt anyone else.

We need more names in black and bold on these pages.

More stories to tell our fellow warriors about to inspire them and teach them to carry on this great tradition.

Do not ever, ever forget the story of Nanette Mikac, begging for the lives of her little girls, or of Martin Bryant shooting those babies at point blank range.

Do not ever forget the story of **ANDY BROWN**, mentally preparing himself to deal with a deadly threat long before he ever faced one, and winning when it counted.

Do not ever forget those little kids at Sandy Hook. Utoya Island. Bath Consolidated School. Cleveland Elementary. Pearl High School. Heath High School. Westside Middle School. Thurston High School. Santee High School. Columbine.

These are our babies. Our little lambs, and there are slobbering jackals trying to drag them off into the darkness and do unspeakable things to them, but they cannot have them. There is a larger, greater, more powerful and noble beast than any terrorist mass shooting rampaging gun-wielding delusional YouTube video recording baby killing booby-trapping attention seeking temper tantrum throwing miniscule meaningless cretin.

There is a thick, proud, strong, historic, true blue line separating the jackals and serpents from the lambs in this nation and that line is defended by lions.

We are those lions and this is, and always will be, our jungle.

SEVEN: Ready Up

I've done three significant things that have helped me prepare to do my part in all this. Things I consider extremely valuable and wanted to share with you here.

First and foremost, I carry off-duty. Religiously. It's taken some adjusting in terms of what I wear and increased my level of awareness in terms of where other people are in relation to my weapon. Pretty much the same thing I've always done at work. Now instead of simply standing in line at the store, playing with my phone, I tend to blade myself so that my gun is away from the people crowding in behind me, or that my arm is covering the gun. Again, this is the same thing we all do, or should do, at work.

I've used a few different off-duty carry methods, depending on what I'm doing or where I'm going. I use the standard hip holster, mainly, and this allows me to maintain continuity with the muscle memory I've developed and trained with over the years.

The only drawback to that is I have to take extra efforts to keep the gun concealed. In the summer time, that usually means a baggier shirt, or an open short sleeved button down shirt, to cover the weapon.

As an alternate to holstering the weapon, I also have a Maxpedition Fatboy Versipack shoulder bag that allows me to stow the gun, as well as my wallet, phone, etc. The drawback to this carry option is that I'm basically walking around with a tactical purse. That, and now retaining the bag is job one, because it has everything I need in it.

In searching for a solution to the hip carry and bag carry options, I purchased a few concealed carry t-shirts, the ones with holsters built into either side under the armpit. I've found that while these offer excellent concealment, especially when combined with a loose-fitting shirt, they are wildly dangerous for the weapon I carry. I carry a Glock, and because I maintain symmetry between on-duty and off-duty weapons, I keep one in the chamber. The fabric of the t-shirt that is supposed to act as a holster is far too thin to provide protection against a misfire. Without an additional holster insert to keep the weapon secure and safe, the t-shirts are simply too dangerous. Even if you carry a gun with an external safety, the lever can be switched off and on through the shirt and the trigger can too-easily be pulled.

The second thing I've done is shoot more. I know it sounds rudimentary and for those of you who are gun guys, you're probably scratching your head in confusion right now saying, "You mean instead of shooting three times a week, you now shoot five, right?"

Wrong.

For most of my career, I only shot twice a year. Once when I qualified and another time that was either training, or begrudgingly going to a range somewhere to make sure I could still hit the damn target before I had to go qualify. I was never, in my entire career, a great shot. I wasn't the worst, but I struggled at times.

It was a source of anxiety, knowing I had to qualify. And I suppose it was a symptom of my anxiety or lack of faith in myself using a gun that caused me to have The Dream. You know the one I mean. The one where you pull the trigger and the bullet plops out of the barrel and falls to the ground. Or the one where someone is coming at you and you draw your weapon and try to fire, but the trigger is too hard to pull.

In the past year I've shot more than I ever have. I know I can make this firearm do what I want it to. I have developed a familiarity and confidence in my weapon and my ability to use it that I never had before.

I've sought out better tactics and adopted new ideas in order to make myself a more effective shooter. It's amazing what you can learn from SWAT guys when you ask them. They are overflowing with information and love to share it.

For instance, I used to shoot from a Weaver stance, because that is how I was trained in the Academy. I learned that I was exposing my entire side to the threat, where the panels of my vest don't meet, and leaving my heart and lungs exposed to being shot.

Now, I shoot from a combat stance. I face the target directly, using the entire front of my vest to protect me, shooting from a crouched forward position to make myself harder to hit. If this were baseball, I'd be giving the pitcher a much smaller strike zone. In addition, I find that by keeping both hands forward and my elbows locked, I'm giving myself a much more stable platform to shoot from.

Lastly, I've put together a bag of essential gear that I might need in order to deal with almost any situation. It is, of course, not completely perfect. I make adjustments all the time, depending on how things are working. I'm always searching for ways to eliminate redundancies, reduce weight, or add items I've overlooked.

There is no perfect science to this. Much smarter, more tactically-minded people will have things in their gear bag, go bag, active shooter bag, or whatever you want to call it, that I do not. This is simply what is in my go bag. This is what I've found that works for me, as of this writing. By next week, I might learn something new, and the entire thing will have changed.

First and foremost, I carry a Maxpedition Condor-II backpack. It's a rugged, double-strapped backpack with multiple PALS webbing options. Just for the record, I'm not connected to Maxpedition in any way. I simply use their products because they suit my purposes, and so far, I've found them to be adequately functional. I would prefer to carry something made in the United States rather than Taiwan, but for now, this is what I have.

I use several attachments to the bag, including: A radio holder, a magazine pouch, and a medical kit. The magazine pouch holds two loaded mags that are easily accessible. The medical kit is a 5.11 Tactical VTAC 6x6 Utility Pouch, attached via PALS webbing, and contains the following items:

- Rubber gloves
- Folding A.G. Russell Cowboy knife
- Surgical tape
- Neosporin
- Lg. gauze pads
- 2 tampons
- Asheman chest seal
- Kendall pentrolatum gauze

- Burn jel
- Antiseptic wipes
- Assorted bandages
- 1st aid cream
- 3-in-1 cream
- Clean wipes
- Tactical tourniquet

Now, a few of you smartasses saw that I put tampons in my medical kit and started snickering, didn't you. Well, let the old dog school you for a second, youngin'. Tampons make excellent puncture wound stoppers. They are designed to be inserted and absorb blood. One of the many benefits of studying knife fighting, especially when you are using a live blade, is that you get many opportunities to dress wounds.

Plus, it is always fun when you are with someone you know is whining about having a bad day and you pull out a tampon and say, "Here, you forgot this."

Moving on.

Inside the bag itself, I keep these items:

- Handcuffs, hinged, Peerless
- Black handkerchief
- Fixed Ka-bar TDI Law Enforcement, small blade, serrated, with holster
- Multi-tool
- Pens/markers
- Paracord bracelet

- Police baseball hat
- Notepad
- 2 boxes of extra ammo
- Badge in neck holder, with a handcuff key hidden inside
- Rubber gloves in a small case
- Large Heckler and Koch fixed blade with sheath
- Interior maps to local schools
- SOG Tactical tomahawk

True story: Everybody laughed at me when I told them I was buying a tactical tomahawk for my go bag, and I started to feel a little self-conscious about it. I thought maybe I was over doing it. I mean, at the time, it made perfect sense to me because a rampage killer might bar the doors like Seung-Hui Cho did at Virginia Tech, and you may need a way to smash through a glass window or entrance. So the tomahawk finally arrived and I sheepishly wound up showing one of my best friends, who happens to be a Seminole Indian as well as a dedicated SWAT operator, and he said, "I have the same exact one in my go bag."

And that, ladies and gentleman, is when you know it is okay to be crazy, because the people you know and respect are crazy right along with you.

EIGHT: Schaffer's Ten Golden Rules of Confidential Informants

My dad spent over thirty years on the job. He retired as sergeant in charge of detectives and as a boss, he still routinely took cases. When he left his PD, his captain gave me a copy of a video from one of his interviews where he gleaned a confession from a suspect. It was interesting to watch the old man work. He had a very conversational style with the suspect, a female, and as the interview wore on, she started sinking lower and lower in her chair, like she was deflating. To his credit, the old man stayed with her though. He pulled his chair in front of her and kept talking, bending forward as he spoke to maintain eye contact with her, going lower and lower until both of them were nearly folded in half.

It was an interesting technique that I've never seen employed anywhere else, and if you asked him about it, he'd shrug and say that's just how it went down. He winged it. Made it up as he went along, which I suspect, was true for much of his style of investigation.

Even though he's only twenty-two years older than I am, and we were both on the job at the same time for around five years, we are completely different police officers whose ideas of the job are completely foreign to one another.

I remember when I was a kid he used to delight in telling me stories about how he conned people. He used to carry a fingerprint card around in his police hat and he'd whip it out and say, "You know how I solved that last case? I found a suspect and when he denied doing it, I showed him this fingerprint and said, 'Then how did I find this at the crime scene?' He just hung his head and gave it up."

He used to tell me stories about how they'd even use the photocopier to get confessions. This is an urban legend in every police department known to man, but these knuckleheads heard about it working in other PDs at the time and decided to try it.

First, they'd feed paper into the photocopier with the words *TRUE* typed across the first three pages and *LIE* typed across the fourth, and they'd bring a suspect in. They'd tell him about their fancy new photocopier that was also calibrated for detecting lies. "Put your hand on the glass here and hold it steady while we ask you a few questions. Is your name Bill Smith?"

Bill would say yes, and my dad would press the copy button. The scanner would go back and forth and a piece of paper would shoot out with Bill's hand printed on it and the word *TRUE* written across the bottom.

My dad would hold up the page and nod and say, "Good, good. Keep that up. Do you work at Joe's mechanic shop?"

Another answer and another page printed out that said, *TRUE.*

Finally, they'd get through the preliminary questions and my dad would say, "Bill, did you break into the safe and steal the week's deposit?"

Bill, of course would deny it, and the copier would spit out another printed image of his hand. My dad would hold it up and show him the word *LIE* printed across the bottom, shaking his head sadly.

Now, the way my dad tells it, every bad guy confessed to this ruse and it worked beautifully, but old cops are like fishermen. They never let the truth get in the way of a good story. All I know is that all the cops crowding behind the one-way mirror watching this display of chicanery was probably too busy pissing their pants laughing to hear if the guy confessed or not.

The most fundamental way my dad and I differ in terms of police work is that he never worked narcotics. To him, illegal street drugs meant marijuana and Quaaludes and not much else. He was simply never interested in it, and his department did not afford him the opportunity or encouragement to become so. In many ways, the older generation of small town police departments avoided pursuing narcotics investigations, because it was easy to say "There are no drugs in this town," if you never found any.

One good way to never find any is to never look.

In the beginning of my career in narcotics, I was able to witness the last stages of cocaine as the major street drug in the Philadelphia region. Normally, we came across eight balls of soft (powder cocaine in one-eighth ounce increments) and that is what we bought, because in the Commonwealth of Pennsylvania, that amount of cocaine qualified the defendant for a mandatory sentence.

But cocaine quickly gave way to pills, mainly due to the arrival of Oxy 80's. Oxy 80's, which are no longer available, were devastating. OxyContin, a brand name for the pills, contained 80 milligrams of

Oxycodone, a synthetic opiate. This is a massively high dosage of Oxycodone, and the pills came with a laughably simplistic protective coating.

I've often said that pharmaceutical drugs are much easier for kids to mentally process because so many of them are already on medication already. After all, we're all taught from an early age that "drugs" are bad. Most children wouldn't give a second thought to smoking a cigarette, let alone snorting a line of coke or shooting up with heroin. Those are "drugs" and we reinforce that they are bad over and over.

But pills? From a doctor? Made by a pharmaceutical company that's approved by the FDA? How bad can that be?

According to an article in the Wall Street Journal dated December 28, 2010, at least twenty-five percent of American children are regularly taking medication. Seven percent of them are taking two different kinds.

It should not have been a surprise that they embraced the idea of taking medication for recreational purposes, or that they viewed it as a less serious threat than street drugs. With Oxy came a resurgence in heroin. Oxy addicts were paying anywhere from $50 to upwards of $90 per pill, and the sheer cost of it drove them to seek out alternative methods of feeding their cravings. Heroin, at $10 a bag, was waiting for them.

Along with the infestation of opiate addicts came skyrocketing numbers of burglaries and thefts across the entire region. I know addicts whose goal was to find one hundred open cars every night and take just $2 in change from them. That would be enough for a bundle of heroin, train fare, and minimal spending cash, the next day.

Finally, the makers of OxyContin realized the harm their product had caused and imposed a tamper-proof coating on their pills and did away with the 80mg configuration. Unfortunately, the damage was already done.

According to an article in Bloomberg, February 4 2012, heroin usage increased an astonishing 79 percent in the United States from 2007 to 2012.

Heroin affects us all. If you do not know someone in your family or circle of friends who is struggling with heroin addiction, or the addiction of one of their loved ones, you are either very lucky or have been purposely kept out of the loop.

One thing I always find interesting is speaking with a heroin addict after they've been in prison long enough to go through withdrawal. Once the illness passes, it is like someone turned the lights back on in their eyes. They begin to gain weight and lost that awful pasty, disease-ridden pallor in their faces. All of them swear they are never going to use again.

I always tell them it will be hard, but I hope they mean it because otherwise, they are going to die.

So, for this section, we are going to talk about what I consider to be the single-most important powerful tool in conducting narcotics investigations. These are my basic rules and guidelines for dealing with confidential informants. As I always point out before I begin these segments, there are many of you reading this who have far greater experience than I do. I do not claim to know everything about drug work, and want to make it clear that these are simply my rules. I borrowed and straight up stole most of them from the cops who taught me the investigative trade. Feel free to do the same. This is what has worked for me.

1. Informants are Essential

On a very good day, you can trash pull your way into a pretty decent investigation. Let's say you get a tip about a drug dealer and after corroborating some of the information, get interested enough to wake up at three in the morning to go steal their trash.

Trash pulls have many benefits aside from finding actual drug evidence. You can get biographical information about who lives in the house, where they work, their phone numbers, and more. Even without actual drugs or paraphernalia, you might get owe sheets or cutting agents or some other type of indication that drugs are being packaged or sold inside the residence. Maybe even enough for a search warrant.

If trash pulls prove ineffective, and all you have is an anonymous tip, you will spend large amounts of time conducting surveillance trying to corroborate the information. If you notice a lot of traffic coming to and from the residence, you might consider doing a car stop on a vehicle as it leaves, in hopes that you'll both find the drugs and flip the person to cooperate. This is risky, because if it goes wrong, your target just became aware that there is an investigation.

The absolute best way to begin any drug investigation is with an informant. Informants are the lifeblood of any narcotics unit. If you are interested in doing this kind of work, you must begin cultivating informants at every available opportunity. Every retail theft suspect is a potential informant. Every traffic stop on a person who is going to lose their license if they get one more ticket is a potential informant. Every person you arrest is a potential informant.

We are going to get into the specifics of what makes for a good and bad informant, but this is the first, most important lesson to learn. Informants are vital to narcotics investigators and you need to be actively looking for them.

2. Good Samaritan Informants are Generally Useless

Some departments pay their informants for their cooperation. Some federal agencies do as well, even going so far as to offer the informant a percentage of the final haul. I have little experience with that because paying them is not an option for me. I am sure there are positive and negative factors to paying them, and greater legal minds than myself could argue them. For the purposes of this discussion, there are only two types of informants.

The ones who are on the hook for something and looking to help themselves, and Good Samaritans.

Every once in a while, somebody will walk into a police station and say, "Drugs are destroying our community and I want to help do something about it. Let me help you take down the bad guys."

These people are lured in by what they've seen on television, or by a truly genuine desire to do good.

It won't work.

Now, there are exceptions to every rule and I am sure there are some cases out there that disprove my statement, however, they are few and far between. I am sure some bosses and DA's and inexperienced investigators might love the idea of a Good Samaritan because you get all the milk for free. A voluntary witness with nothing to dirty him up on the stand, who can magically enter the drug world and successfully buy vast sums of narcotics.

Keep dreaming.

For a good CI to work, they need two things. Proper motivation, and experience with the underworld. The life of a CI is hard, ladies and gentlemen. We are sending them off to betray people they know, to assist in police operations, to collect evidence, to potentially testify in court, and to live with the effects of their cooperation. And normally, it's an ongoing process. For someone to stick with it, something very important has to be at stake. I have yet to see a Good Samaritan comply with the level of control an investigator needs to have on a CI.

Second, for as much as the idea of a virginal do-gooder traipsing down the primrose path to lead us all to tractor trailers full of heroin, it simply isn't going to happen. They wouldn't know where to start. In their mind, we're all standing around going, "Okay, boys, we've almost got everything we need to make the bust of a lifetime on Al Capone. If only we knew somebody willing to go in and buy a dimebag of weed!"

If a Good Samaritan wants to cooperate with the police as an informant, my advice is that you thank them for their interest and ask them to be your eyes and ears on the street. Give them your email address and tell them to keep you posted about anything nefarious going on. Most of the time, you will never hear from them again, but it never hurts to try.

3. CIs are Snitches, Liars, and Criminals

You might wind up spending a lot of time with various CI's, whether it is in a professional setting or just the two of you in a car. It is imperative you maintain professional distance from them.

Do not discuss personal details of your life or the people in it.

Do not discuss other investigations or targets.

Do not educate them as to who drug investigations are conducted or what your next step is going to be.

CI's are manipulative people and what you think is just making conversation, they are stowing away for future use. The same way you debriefed them about drug targets once, a bigger, scarier bad guy will be debriefing them about you.

Always play by the rules and document everything, because as surely as a CI will rat on his friends, he will rat on you and your team if anything goes wrong.

These people are not your friends, they are not members of the department, and they are not to be trusted. They are temporary, volatile assets, and they must be controlled.

4. Drug Addicted CIs Will Go Bad Quick So Use them Fast

The sad reality of drug addiction, particularly with opiates, is that it is incredibly hard to overcome. Some people are able to stop using for the rest of their lives, but many others will spend whatever time they have left on the planet in a revolving door of addiction, prison, rehab, and struggling to stay sober. Most of the addicts I deal with actually met the people they were getting high with now in rehab or NA meetings. I mean, at least everybody there knows they have something in common, right?

Addicts are incredibly useful CIs because they spend a large amount of time seeking out drugs. They know fifteen different people to get them from because this is how they spend their life, sending out text message after text message asking if a dealer is good or if they can come through. They normally have everyone in their phone, with all sorts of incriminating conversations.

The problem is, they are probably getting high during their time working for you, regardless of what they say. And even if they are trying to stay clean, that monster is just waiting for them around the corner. When you have a drug addict CI, use them as quickly as you can and be prepared to move on.

I've seen narcotics teams base their entire operation around one CI that the department, and other departments, share for an extended period of time. If someone is viable and productive, continue to use them, however, you must always be ready for the contingency of them going off the reservation and never returning. Your ultimate goal is to work from a CI to a target, flip that target and make them into a CI, get yourself a new target, and repeat that process all over, ad infinitum.

5. Leadeth Not the CI to Targets

Sometimes, I imagine having this conversation with a CI. It starts the way most of them normally do, with me asking, "So what can you do?"

"I don't know. Who do you have in mind?"

"Nobody. Everybody. Start talking."

"Well, do you have anyone in mind you want me to go after?"

"Nope. It's all about what you bring to the table."

"Have you ever heard of Big Mama Schaffer?"

"Nope."

"I'm pretty sure she's your mom."

Then I'm shaking my head, saying, "Doesn't sound familiar."

"Dude, she gave birth to you!"

"Never heard of her."

I don't tell CI's a damn thing about who I know, what I know, or where I know it from. As far as they are concerned, I must be the stupidest drug investigator who ever lived, and that is okay. This accomplishes two things for me.

First, it allows me to hear the CI's information in a pure and direct way, without me filling in the blanks and influencing them. I document their information as if I am hearing it for the first time, no matter how many times I've heard it before. Ultimately, a judge is going to read that information and be able to see that the person being accused was a legitimate target, because so many different people said the same thing about him. Regardless of the amount of narcotics you purchase from a target with a deep history of neighbor complaints and reports from CIs, the court will view him as someone not to take lightly.

Second, that CI is probing me. They're probing the extent of hard won information that may prove extremely useful someday.

It's important to set your ego aside at that point, especially when some 100 pound heroin addict rolls his eyes at you and says, "You must be an idiot because everybody knows that guy."

Our job as investigators is never, ever, to give out information that we know. Our job is to take it in. Your CI will be more productive if they are working on targets they already know anyway. Your job is to find out who they know, how well they know them, and which ones take priority.

6. Keep Your CI within Their Range

One of the most important questions you can ask your CI is how much they normally buy. If they are a two bag a day buyer, it's going to look damn odd if they walk in and ask for a rack of heroin. If they normally do a dimebag of weed on Friday, it's going to raise a few red flags if they suddenly want sixteen pounds of marijuana.

Normally, it isn't even necessary to buy vast quantities of drugs. You will still get enough for an arrest warrant, or search warrant, and be able to seize the supply anyway. Investigators need to have a firm understanding of the weights and mandatory sentences that apply in their state. It makes no sense to spend large amounts of money to buy exciting sounding quantities of drugs if you don't successfully enter a new level of mandatory sentencing.

Listen, everybody wants to make the big haul. Everybody wants to stand there and wave around bricks of drugs and say, "Look at how much we took off the street!"

That's great, and when it happens, be proud, because those investigations invariably take a lot of time, resources, and effort. Do not mess up a good, solid distribution case where you can buy two bags of heroin at a shot from a dealer by trying to force them into giving you quantity.

7. Properly Debrief CI's about Each Target

It's easy to debrief a CI about the first name they give you. Even the second. But remember, most addicts can rattle off multiple names of potential targets just by scrolling through their phones. In the first instance you might learn everything about a target there is to know, from where he lives and what he likes to order at McDonalds. By the fifth, you're writing down, "Steve. Sells heroin."

Look over some of your better CI debriefings and compile a form based on the information you needed, whether during operations, or when you were writing your affidavits, or at trial. Always direct your inquiries toward gaining corroborative information that will eventually help you in your search and arrest warrants.

For instance, a CI tells you Steve is a white male who sells heroin and cocaine. Steve uses his cellphone to make the arrangements and calls the heroin "diesel" and the cocaine "girl." You later have the CI text Steve and say, "need 2 diesel."

Steve, in this imaginary scenario where drug dealers are prompt and reliable service providers, immediately writes back, "Come thru."

You document all of this, including photographing the text messages and the number they were sent to. Sure enough, you make a controlled buy and receive two small wax baggies containing heroin. You've now corroborated the CI's information and can proceed in your investigation easily. By getting the proper information on your target, you are laying the foundation of a proper case that will stand up in any court.

Here are a few tips on information you should consider asking:

- All biographical data on the target, including who they are, where they live, where they work, what they drive, and more.
- What is the CI's history with the target, including all drug activity. How many times has the CI bought, when is the last time the CI bought, what has the CI bought, and what were the quantities and cost?
- What is the target's terminology for what they sell?
- Where does the target keep his stash, money, and weapons?
- Who is the target's supplier? Has the CI ever met the supplier?
- Has the CI ever introduced other buyers to the target?
- What other crimes is the target involved in, and what else do we need to know before meeting this person?
- Once the CI has provided this information gather all previous reports about the target, their criminal history, and see if you can introduce any historical information about their narcotics involvement into your new case.

In addition to gathering information about the targets, you are also going to have to learn about your CI. For instance, if they are going to be driving a car, do they have a good driver's license? That may sound like an inconsequential item, but let's imagine that the CI has a suspended driver's license for being DUI. While he's involved in one of your operations and driving his own car, he gets in a car accident and hurts someone.

Do you want to be on the stand explaining how your drug investigation was so important you let a DUI-Suspended motorist drive and cripple a kid?

No, I think not. It is never a good idea to get so consumed with an operation that you do something stupid or rush in without thinking it over.

No drug investigation is worth your career, or the health and safety of your team, or the welfare of the people we are sworn to protect and serve. Yes, that includes drug dealers and CIs.

8. When a CI Goes Bad, Cut them Loose

Just like in any relationship, if the CI goes bad and you take them back, you have taught them one thing: They can get away with it.

I'm not saying you have to introduce a policy of zero tolerance with these people, because you have to bear in mind, they are generally screw-ups and drug addicts. Have a little wiggle room set aside for the regular stuff that was not done maliciously. Of course, never tell them that. And when you find out they screwed up, you have to get in their face and scream at them. Make sure that they totally understand that any more violations of your CI agreement will not only get them booted out of the program but they will lose any credit they might have built up by working for you.

As I said before, the faster you use them and lose them, the better off you are, particularly when they start to revert back to old ways.

What I'm talking about by "going bad" is when a CI is caught making a buy not under your supervision, or breaking the law, or stealing, or lying. I don't care if they are on the verge of handing you Pablo Escobar, cancel their involvement. Do not necessarily tell them that, but do not use them for future operations because once you have official knowledge that they are back on the dark side, you cannot risk the integrity of your case to be compromised by having them involved.

If your entire case revolved around the CI's cooperation and you can't move forward without them, cut your losses and charge with what you have, regardless of what bigger fish they promise to haul in. Those fish will always be out there, friend. No need to go after them with bad bait.

9. Keep Your Word

As a rule, you should always keep your word and treat people with respect, and this is true of dealing with CIs as well. It's not as easy as it sounds. When you are stuck in a car with someone who has not bathed or changed clothes in over a week, it can be difficult, but remember that you are a professional and they are a civilian. Act like it.

Most heroin addicts are used to being called names by the cops. Cops belittle them and act like they are riddled with contagious diseases. Bear that in mind when you meet someone and offer them something to drink, or ask them how they are feeling. Ask them about their illness and remember they are a real person, not some caricature of a junkie.

One thing I always tell a CI is that I will do what I say, whether it is good or bad. If I tell you I will arrest you and revoke your status if you screw up, I will do it. If I tell you I will show up at court and advocate on your behalf, based on the amount of work you do, then I will do that too.

People talk. They talk to their fellow heroin addicts, they talk to their defense attorneys, and those defense attorneys talk to each other as well. If you keep your word and never screw over an informant, word will get out. If you laugh it off and figure you got what you came for and have already moved on to bigger and better things, that will get out too.

An easy way to keep your word with a CI is to never promise them anything you cannot deliver. Do not tell them they'll never testify, and do not make assurances about what the DA's office or a judge might do with their charges. That is not up to you.

Typically, CIs will want the maximum amount of credit for the least amount of work. You must very quickly relieve them of that mistaken belief and tell them that they will get credit for the work that they do. The amount they get depends on how much they do and how well they do it.

A quick word about defense attorneys, especially ones who specialize in defending narcotics cases.

I love them.

Not necessarily in a jury trial, but if a potential CI tells me he wants to bring his attorney with him, I always say, "Perfect." An experienced defense attorney knows his job will be a thousand times easier if his client cooperates, and he'll be able to work all sorts of magic when it comes to sentencing. Also, defense attorneys are excellent at keeping their clients reined in. If the CI starts moving off the reservation, I call their attorney and say, "Your guy is about to blow it."

Normally, I'll get a call back from the attorney in a day or so and everything will have been worked out with the CI. Just like on the street, your reputation will speak volumes about you in the world of drug investigations.

10. Your CI Today is Your Target Tomorrow

One of my favorite sayings is, "Do not educate CIs." The reason for that is simple. Just because someone is acting in the capacity of a confidential informant today does not mean they will not be selling drugs to support their habit tomorrow. Many heroin and pill addicts, especially ones who have to travel to a certain area to score narcotics, will also sell them to the people back home in order to supplement their habit. Some are actually paid in dope and are simply acting as the middle man between the customer and the other addicts.

Under no circumstances should CIs be present while you are planning your operation or briefing your team. All they need to know is what they are instructed to do. Secure them in a separate area where they cannot get into anything and make sure they cannot access any of your operation materials or your case file.

Do not discuss the logistics of your surveillance or how you will be keeping tabs on them. They will ask. Normally, CIs are concerned about how close help will be if they get found out. They also are anxious to know when you are going to arrest the target because they fear being found out. Or, they might just ask because it is interesting and they are curious about the process.

Give them their instructions and tell them to focus on their part. If they are nervous, make like any good football coach would do and tell them you believe in them and know they can get it done. These are people who may not have gotten much encouragement in their lives. It's a good way to get results and good way to deflect them from asking anymore questions.

I don't mean to sound so negative in reference to addicts. I have known several who managed to overcome their addiction and move on to have productive lives. I believe it is a struggle for them to stay clean, but what the hell, it's a struggle for me to not eat six hamburgers sometimes. We all have things we struggle with, and I am extremely proud of the addicts I've known and worked with who have gone on to have jobs and raise families.

I hope they look back on their time with me as worthwhile and a thing that led them in the right direction. Even if they still have no idea how I conducted any of the drug operations.

NINE: America Now

Recently, I took a trip into the mountains of Pennsylvania, going way out into Sullivan County where you see homes that have no running water or electricity. It's about twenty degrees colder up in the mountains, and people move at a different pace. There is a natural spring in the small town of Lopez that runs out along the side of the road and you can stop and drink from it. It runs all year long, gushing out the clearest, cleanest water you could ever taste.

There are 60,000 acres of game land up there, filled with bear, snakes, coyotes, deer, and more. When it gets dark, man, it's gets dark. And it doesn't take long before you can get yourself properly lost. It's good hunting country, good ATV country, and you can't get any cellphone service, so it's good shut-off-the-incessant-interference country, too.

It's the kind of place people fire their guns off from the back porch and nobody minds. In fact, one day we started shooting and before you know it, shots were echoing from every direction, coming from distant homes where the people inside heard us shooting and could not help but join in the fun.

What there isn't, are any cops. Or fire stations. Or ambulance bays. If you get in an emergency situation, you'd better hope someone is around to hear you call for help, because you sure as hell aren't going to be able to call 911 with no service on your cellphone. And even if you do, good luck telling them what tangled pocket of the woods you are stuck in.

It really made me wonder about some of the people we deal with on a regular basis. They don't seem to be able to tie their own shoes without calling for the police to come and help. What would happen to them if they were suddenly dropped in the middle of nowhere, far away from all the support systems modern society has crafted in order to allow them to live a life of complete leisure? Would they find that missing piece of self-reliance we seem to have lost?

In the old days, this country was a lot harder to live in. We had to grow our own food and mend our own clothes. We had to fix our own roofs and look after our own communities. And it worked beautifully. Americans were hard-working, earnest people who achieved amazing things in a short period of time.

Then again, according to the Center for Disease control, the death rate for American citizens aged 1-4 years old declined 94 percent from 1935 to 2010. In fact, the overall mortality rate for Americans declined 60 percent. So, for all our lamentation about how good we had it back in the day, it sure is nice to see all these little kids running around.

Where are we going now?

I will turn 40 this year, and maybe I'm just getting nostalgic in my old age, but things certainly seem different than they used to. Obviously, the world has gotten much larger and faster than it has ever been before. Modern technology has allowed all of us to exist in a kind of simultaneous state with the entire planet. We all physically live in various cities and towns, but at the same time our virtual presence in the great omnisphere of cyberspace allows us to interact, socialize, share, terrorize, romance, and prey on any other person, no matter where they are.

Mastery of this technology has evened the playing field, in many ways, between governments, anarchists, cops, criminals, the rich, and the impoverished.

Pedophiles can network all across the planet in order to ply their loathsome trade, while Amber Alerts can be broadcast across every digital device in a designated area to deploy hundreds of thousands of people to find an abducted child.

Organized crime rings in Somalia, Canada, and Eastern Europe can target elderly victims in America and swindle them out of their life's savings, and our current laws and resources do not afford us the opportunity to do anything more than take a report. But by the same token, a family struggling to pay their child's hospital bill can set up a fundraising site, or conduct their own research into experimental procedures that result in a cure.

I remember when I was a kid I was interested in becoming a federal agent, but I had no idea how to go about it. I looked through the phone book in the government listings and sent letters to every local office asking them how to join their agency. It was time-consuming, cumbersome work, and when the few responses I received in the mail came, they weren't particularly clarifying.

Now, all of that information is only a few keystrokes away. There's a lot of bad and a lot of good, and it probably evens out in the end.

In fact, my entire writing and publishing career is based on technology. Before the advent of Amazon's Kindle and other eReading platforms, I was still like all the other struggling authors out there, sending off query letters to agents, tweaking short stories in hopes of getting them accepted into some fancy-pants literary journal. Technology has allowed me to cut out the middle man. I can write a book about anything I want and offer it directly to the world. It's the readers who decide whether it's worth buying or not.

The good news, or maybe the bad, depending how you look at it, is that things will basically stay the same. Governments will change, borders will shift, societies will come and go, but for as long as there are people on this planet and the Sun does not go supernova, this is essentially it. Old people will lament about the long gone days of yore when things were better before all these damn kids started ruining everything, young people will rebel against a system they perceive is keeping them down and the old fogies clutching to power with their withered, liver-spotted hands. Technology can change all it likes, but at the end of the day, humans behave no differently than we did in ancient times, and I see no reason to believe we will behave differently for many generations to come.

Of course, there are always those who will tell you it is getting worse. For instance, there's this guy:

"The young people of today think of nothing but themselves. They have no reverence for parents or old age. They are impatient of all restraint. They talk as if they alone knew everything and what passes for wisdom with us is foolishness with them. As for girls, they are forward, immodest and unwomanly in speech, behavior and dress."

Or

"The children now love luxury. They have bad manners, contempt for authority, they show disrespect to their elders.... They no longer rise when elders enter the room. They contradict their parents, chatter before company, gobble up dainties at the table, cross their legs, and are tyrants over their teachers."

The first quote is attributed to Hesiod, a Greek poet in 750 BC, and was believed to have first been inscribed on an Ancient Egyptian tomb. The second is attributed to either Socrates or Plato, nobody is sure, but at the very least we can say that it is damn old. There are multiple examples throughout history of the older generation complaining about the next one, calling them lazy and spoiled. We do it now, especially when we are talking about police officers. Nearly every police supervision text book or article you read today mentions something about the way Generation Y, or Millennials, approach things from a different point of view, are less militaristic, or (God forbid) want to know why they are being told to do something.

In my opinion, all those articles are just reinforcement for administrators who've grown too set in their ways and too lazy to lead by example, to really be out there in the ranks doing the work. The work is what keeps you young, or at the very least, aware of the real world. I've always felt that the best way to know what your people are doing is to be out there doing it with them, at least every once in a while, as time allows.

From the year 2000 to 2013, there were over 30 predictions the world would end, coming from such luminaries as Jerry Falwell, Pat

Robertson, the Hermetic Order of the Golden Dawn, and Rasputin. Even the great Isaac Newton thought we'd bite the dust in 2000.

Nope.

No rapture, no apocalypse, no alien invasion. For anyone convinced it is going to happen, I openly encourage them to send me all of their money and real estate holdings, just so they can enter the new world divested of such unwanted earthly material possessions. So far, no takers.

It would be very easy for me to end this book on a paranoid, sky-is-falling note that spoke to our worst fears and suspicions. Many people have formed entire franchises around scaring others into believing the end is nigh. Hell, I could sell you books, bunkers, canned goods, weapons, and everything I tell you that you'll need to survive after the asteroid hits.

I think, by far, the scarier and harder to accomplish reality is that life will go on. How it goes on, however, is up to us. If we spend all our time stockpiling food, waiting for the lights to go out and the government to fail, there will be mass shootings committed by rampage killers every other week. We'll be too busy focused on an imaginary event to realize that nobody is minding the farm. We will have given up.

If we can dig deep to find the resolve within ourselves to protect what we have, to keep it from slipping away, then we can safely and proudly turn over this planet to our children. To safeguard this world and this society so that someday, they will look back on our efforts and feel the same gratitude we feel for our grandfathers who fought in WWII.

America's best days are not over. They are ahead of us, but like anything else, that is a journey we must undertake together. It won't be handed to us. It won't rain down from the sky because we're special. It must be sought after. It must be found. It must be won.

What we're really talking about are values. Old school, die hard American values. Only, not the ones that everyone thinks.

The concept of values has been hijacked by people who truly misunderstand, or misappropriate, what they mean. They claim the country has lost its way by becoming less fundamentalist. They want us to be more race specific, gender specific, and class specific. *All this abortion and gay marriage and interracial breeding and socialized health care is leading us straight to hell, which is why God is going to smite the United States of America the first chance he gets.*

What they don't say, or simply do not know, is that the idea of God encroaching on government operations is a relatively new concept.

For instance, "In God We Trust" is a famous symbol that appears on the most important documents in American society: Our money. And yet, that phrase was not adopted by the United States until 1956. Up until then, we used the phrase "E pluribus unum," which translates as, "Out of many, one."

The reason we adopted it in the Fifties was to distinguish ourselves from the Soviet Union, who promoted statewide atheism.

Even the phrase "One nation, under God" in the Pledge of Allegiance was not added until 1954. Up until then, from 1892, when the pledge was first composed, we were simply one nation, indivisible.

One old saw people love to roll out in times of trouble is that When They Took Prayer Out of Public Schools, All This Trouble Started. Not true. Prayer in public schools was banned in 1962 by the Supreme Court, who ruled it unconstitutional. The pundits say that when we banned God, we invited our own destruction. The thinking, I suppose, is that back then God loved us enough to keep our children safe from rampage killers, but now, not so much.

Except we know that Andrew Philip Kehoe killed 44 people, most of them children, back in 1927. The Galveston hurricane killed approximately 8,000 people in 1900. The attack on Pearl Harbor in 1941 killed over 2,400. The Johnstown Flood in 1889 killed 2,209. I could rattle off dozens of examples of massive tragedies that have struck this country time and time again, regardless of whether or not we allowed prayer in school or gay marriage at the time.

Anyone who says differently is simply lying. Or they're trying to scare you. More than likely, they want you to send them money right away in order to help stop our collective plunge down the toilet of history.

Sumbitch, first he goes after the NRA and now he's picking on sweet baby Jesus. This boy's gone too far now...

Truly, I have no qualms with people of religious faith. Some of you may hold your faith and convictions very deeply, and I am not belittling them. Fortunately, for you and me, the founding fathers of this country allowed the chance to all of us to believe in whatever we chose. Of course, as long as it did not interfere with governance of the United States.

If you are truly looking for some traditional, fundamental American values, I invite you to look no further than the Constitution and Bill of Rights. Imagine a country that was truly guided by the precepts of Life, Liberty, and the Pursuit of Happiness for each individual citizen. That is a vision that has sparked great love for America all around the world and caused people from every nation to want to come here. That is what has made us the great shining city upon a hill, and if we can agree that concept, that country, is worth preserving, then we can agree it is worth fighting for.

You and I do not have to agree on many things, and perhaps we don't, but let us agree on that.

In 1970, American sociologist Robin Williams (No, not Mork. Or the genie, for you younger kids.) defined what American values really are. Williams was no lightweight academic. He served on the front lines in WWII. According to Cornell Universities obituary, Williams served in the European Theater of Operations and the Special Services from '42 to '46. His special insight into what our boys went through in that war led him to later publish the authoritative work on the lives of soldiers, from recruitment to combat, called, fittingly, The American Soldier.

Soldier, scholar, teacher, when people talk about The Greatest Generation, Williams was in the thick of it. If a man like that tells us what American values are, I think we owe him a listen. According to Mr. Williams, our core values are:

- Equal Opportunity
- Achievement and Success
- Material Comfort
- Activity and Work
- Practicality and Efficiency
- Progress
- Science
- Democracy and Enterprise
- Freedom

Commitment to those key values are what kept the country strong through its worst times of the past century. We need to raise those principles back up as standards worth achieving and overcome this short-sighted, superstitious wave of paranoia that's swept through too many of our communities and schools.

Like most people interested in the victory of science and reasoning over demagoguery, I paid very close attention to the debate between Bill Nye and Ken Hamm over the scientific viability of Creationism. I'll offer no opinions about the subject, except to say that Bill Nye uttered one key word that not only struck to the very heart of the matter, it should have rung like a bell for every single criminal investigator alive on the planet.

First, the debate's moderator asked Hamm what it would take to change his mind about his belief, and he said that nothing could.

They asked Mr. Nye the same question and he responded that all it would take is evidence.

Evidence, ladies and gentlemen. The cornerstone of our very trade and function. So, for all of the naysayers and doomsdayers and cynics who say this country, and even this world, is on the downward spiral, I will tell you that the evidence does not support that.

It has always been hard. And dangerous. And deadly. The weak have always been at the mercy of the vicious, but I guarantee you that people living in any other time period have never known the kind of safety and peace that we enjoy right now. These are freedoms that were too hard fought for, and too hard won, for us to allow them to be maligned by charlatans and cult leaders and snake handlers and lobbyists who tell us we're doomed.

If you look at Mr. Williams's nine core American values, you can clearly see that every internal struggle this country has ever faced has been for one or more of those things. Every struggle we face now is for the same thing. But instead of the majority accepting those demanding equal opportunity and freedom, or using that as an opportunity to teach our children that is what makes America so strong, I see cowardice. I see fear. I see it in some of your eyes reading this right now.

I challenge you, that if you truly love this country and the principles she was founded on, if you truly believe in that brilliantly shining city upon the hill, you must be brave enough to grow and to change.

According to a May 3, 2014, article in The Economist, America does not strike fear in the hearts of our enemies anymore, and our allies are not sure we can protect them any longer. It describes how Russia is seizing land in the Ukraine, China is pushing surrounding countries out of their own waters, and Syria is killing its own people at will. Everywhere we look, other countries are growing larger, richer, stronger, and more bold. All we hear about is how China, Russia, India, etc., are on their way to becoming the New Superpower.

Yet, the citizens of these so called New Superpowers lack the fundamental dignities and protection that are commonplace here.

India, where the head of a village in West Bengal can order the gang rape of a 20-year-old woman, just because she was in a relationship with a man from somewhere else.

Russia, where a former KGB agent can be made Acting President, then serve two terms as President, leave the Presidency due to term limits and become Prime Minister who rules in tandem with a puppet-president, then have the law changed to make the President's term six years instead of four, just in time for him to come back and be President again.

Russia, who has seen fit to criminalize homosexuality. Russia, who has reasserted Soviet-era control over media. Russia, where anyone they term a "foreign agent" can vanish at the drop of a hat.

And let us not forget China.

According to the Office of the United States Trade Representative, China is our largest supplier of imported goods. We export $141 billion dollars' worth of goods to the Chinese, but import a whopping $429 billion. Our electronics, machinery, furniture, toys and sneakers are all coming from China, and they are our third largest supplier of agricultural products.

Imagine that for a moment.

According to a ten-year study by Timothy Jones, a University of Arizona anthropologist working for the Bureau of Applied Research in Anthropology, stated that the United States of America disposes of half of the food we produce here.

According to a NY Times article dated May 29, 2013, the previous year we imported 4.1 billion tons of food from China. Imports included tuna, oranges, mushrooms, apple juice, and much, much more. And yet we destroy half of what is grown here.

There are other costs of doing business with the Chinese. While the United States Federal minimum wage is $7.25 an hour, the Chinese operate "Reprimand Centers" where people being imprisoned indefinitely are forced to make many of the $429 billion dollars' worth of those goods we import.

The crushing reality of who we're doing business with pops up in strange ways sometimes. In 2007, China had to recall over a million toys that were coated with lead paint, potentially poisoning our children.

In 2012, a woman in the Portland area opened a box of Halloween decorations she'd bought at K-Mart and found a letter from a Chinese prisoner. According to an article from The Oregonian, dated December 23, 2012, the letter described thousands of people being forced to work in the Masanjia Labor Camp in Shenyang.

A Huffington Post article dated April 29, 2014, a woman in New York found another letter from a Chinese prisoner in a pair of rain boots she bought at Saks Fifth Avenue.

And for those not enslaved at labor camps, working in Chinese factories is hardly better.

In July, 2012, China Labor Watch reported that 18 workers committed suicide at Foxconn factories in a period of two years. Foxconn is the largest private employer in China and at the time were the main manufacturer of Apple products.

In March, 2013, Apple distanced itself from Foxconn and took up with a company called Pegatron, due to all the controversy. Pegatron was soon found to be committing multiple human rights abuses as well. On December 11, 2013, the NY Times reported that a 15-year-old boy had dropped dead of pneumonia after working 12 hours days on the assembly line of a plant making Apple iPhones.

This is but a mere glimpse at the countries around the world we are not only doing business with, but are competing with, for economic power and decision-making ability on the world stage.

In July 2011, Syrian-American composer Malek Jandali performed *Watani Ana (I am my Homeland)* in Lafayette Park, across from the White House. At the time, the Arab Spring was in full swing and Jandali has been a vocal supporter of the movement. According to a CNN article dated July 30, 2011, Jandali's parents were targeted by Syrian governmental security forces and beaten almost to death. They knocked his 66-year-old mother's teeth out, taunting her that they were going to "teach" her how she should have raised her son.

Jendali continued to perform and be outspoken, and according to a follow-up CNN article written that September, the Syrian security forces returned to the family home. Except the parents were already gone.

They'd fled to the United States.

America, you see, is not a place comprised of Republicans and Democrats. It's not a place occupied by heterosexuals and homosexuals. It is not a place populated by either NRA-supporters or gun-control advocates. Pro-life or pro-choice supporters. Black people or white people. Us or Them.

It's only a place made up of, and by, Americans. It is what we make it, year after year, decade after decade, century after century.

When those Chinese prisoners hide letters meant for people here to read, it is like a marooned sailor sending a message in a bottle out into the sea. Except, the prisoners are sending their pleas for freedom to the one place they know will respond. They are reaching out across the great divides of faith, culture, and civilization, taking greater risk than we can ever imagine, because they believe in who we are and what we stand for.

When people like Malek Jandali stand up to cry out against injustice, regardless of their loved one's safety, or their own, they are sending that message back out into world and telling them we hear you loud and clear. We understand. We know.

America, as a country, can do better. We as Americans can work harder. We can find ways to contribute, and volunteer, and get our hands dirty in continuing this great legacy. As we learn and grow as individuals and take the time to strengthen those around us, in committing ourselves to those essential American core values and clearing the path for others to do the same, so does the country.

And all it takes to get it done is you. All it takes to get it started is doing it right now.

Someone once told me that police officers are the first, most obvious representative of the government to the public. I wouldn't know a tax collector or zoning official if I saw them in the street, or probably most of the Senators or State Representatives if I was behind them in the supermarket, but cops? Cops are easy to spot with their uniforms and marked cars, and if you can't find one, they're just a quick phone call away.

We already know that people hold us all accountable for what cops do in other parts of the country. They'll lump dirty cops from whatever fleabitten backwater rat hole of a town who got caught doing something illegal and act like everybody patrolling their neighborhood is just as guilty. I think in some ways, the actions of government reflect on us just as well.

The answer, obviously, is that the police officer is such a strong symbol, an icon that runs deep in the American consciousness. We've been immortalized talking to the little runaway boy in the Norman Rockwell painting. In photographs of the older officer seen tying a little kid's sneakers. NYPD Officer Larry DePrimo buying boots for a homeless man who was barefoot on a winter night. The Boston cops reacting instantly at the sound of explosions at the Marathon. The heroes running in and out of the World Trade Center as it collapsed.

Those are the cops I want to be. Those are the cops I look up to. And if the world looks to the people of the United States of America for inspiration, and if the people of the United States look to her police officers as the first and most immediate representative of the government, we owe it to them to give them something worth believing in.

Old cops, such as I am quickly becoming, like to kid one another about how idealistic we were back when we started. We laugh that we wanted to "make a difference," sneering when we say those words like they are tinged with sulfur. We sigh heavily and accept that our cynicism has worn us all thin and too many years of dealing with people has stripped us of our capacity to care about helping them.

If you let it, the long parade of victims and doers and crazies and scumbags and junkies and drunks and all the people who are directly responsible for their own misfortune begin to blur together. They all get neatly categorized in the "Them" category, while we sit firmly in the "Us" category. It's a way to distance ourselves from what others go through. It's also a very effective way of dehumanizing whole groups of people, until it no longer seems important to care about what happens to them.

Every time you go the extra mile for someone in need, every time you follow up with a victim to make sure they are doing all right, every time you remove a threat to a child's life, every time you are walking your beat and getting to know the people you protect and serve, you are investing in this country with your time and your energy instead of just collecting a paycheck. It's worth investing in. And it's worth protecting.

We will continue to face difficult challenges in the years to come. Prepare for them. Train for them. Equip yourself for them. When they come, the lions like you and I will be ready. One nation. Indivisible. With liberty and justice for all.

Bernard Schaffer is the author of multiple books that span a wide variety of genres, including literature, police procedurals, and science fiction westerns. He has worked on several projects with famous authors such as Harlan Ellison, Alan Dean Foster, and Bill Thompson (the editor who discovered Stephen King and John Grisham).

Recently, he collaborated with J.A. Konrath on two books that feature Konrath's best-selling Lt. Jack Daniels characters, and ones from Schaffer's own Superbia series.

A lifelong resident of the Philadelphia area, he is the proud father of two children.

For More Information about Bernard Schaffer

Official Website and Newsletter Info!

The Bernard Schaffer Author Facebook Fan Page

Email: ApiarySociety@gmail.com

Twitter: @BernardSchaffer

Receive a Personalized Authorgraph for this Book!

Bernard Schaffer is a proud participant in the Authorgraph program, which allows readers to request a personalized note for any of the listed books. Simply click the above link and be sure to mention a few things about yourself. You will receive a response shortly thereafter!

Also Available from Bernard Schaffer

Superbia 1

Superbia 2

Superbia 3

Cheese Wrestling (w/ J.A. Konrath)

Snake Wine (w/ J.A. Konrath)

Way of the Warrior

Way of the Warrior 2

Guns of Seneca 6

Old-Time Lawmen

Magnificent Guns of Seneca 6

Immaculate Killers

Grendel Unit 1: Bad Day at Kor-Wa

Grendel Unit 2: Ignition Sequence

Grendel Unit and Far From Home: Sun Hammer 2

Whitechapel: The Final Stand of Sherlock Holmes

The Girl from Tenerife

Women and Other Monsters

Overdogs

Agent Omega: You Only Live Forever

Thirsty Blade

The Manifesto of Independent Writing and Publishing

Also available: Billionaire's Apprentice, by Chase Carroway

Way of the Warrior 2

Bernard Schaffer

Published by Dia de los Toros Publications

Edited by Laurie Laliberte

38329470R10124

Made in the USA
Lexington, KY
03 January 2015